Lust, Lucre & Liquor
and
Piece of Work

Lust, Lucre & Liquor

and

Piece of Work

▼

Brad Field

Writers Club Press
San Jose New York Lincoln Shanghai

Lust, Lucre & Liquor and Piece of Work

All Rights Reserved © 2001 by Brad S Field

No part of this book may be reproduced or transmitted in any form or by any means, graphic, electronic, or mechanical, including photocopying, recording, taping, or by any information storage retrieval system, without the permission in writing from the publisher.

Writers Club Press
an imprint of iUniverse.com, Inc.

For information address:
iUniverse.com, Inc.
5220 S 16th, Ste. 200
Lincoln, NE 68512
www.iuniverse.com

ISBN: 0-595-15045-4

Printed in the United States of America

Lust, Lucre, and Liquor
and
Piece of Work
Two Plays

Lust, Lucre, and Liquor is the kind of play that people produce for the fun of it. No one would do it for any other reason. The play offers to some prospective producers—at first glance—one grave difficulty: there are five acts, with three scenes in each act—a total of fifteen scenes—with a set-change every scene. But a quick and efficient method of accommodating any proscenium stage to these demands is outlined at the end of this text of the play, with illustrations. The "roll-drops" described there are fun to build, fun to look at, fun to act in front of, and contribute to the tone of owlishly solemn tackiness appropriate to any production of "Lust."

The play, with the sets described at the end, runs about 60 to 70 minutes, allowing for no intermission and for an average of thirty seconds for set changes—that is, ten seconds for some, none longer than fifty seconds. The first scene of act IV requires getting the "saw" on-stage and off at the end, so those two scene-changes my be appropriately covered by duets by members of the cast, singing in front of the curtain, "No, No, A Thousand Times No" for one change, and "She's More to be Pitied than Censured" for the other. Quick set-changes are the result of practice, just as rapid pick-up of line cues in the dialogue. The ten-second set change, say from a woods to a barroom, is a nice comic effect. The audience sees the act-curtain rattle shut, and while the curtain is still swinging, hears the squeak of pulleys as the wood-drop is rolled up and the thump as the bar-drop unrolls and its hits the stage floor. In same ten seconds, the actors, who had been waiting in the wings with the appropriate pieces, put out the table, the two chairs, the pained Masonite set-piece that represents the bar. The curtain whips open again. The suddenness of the switch often gets a laugh. More important, the tempo of the piece is not allowed to sag. Rehearsing the changes again and again is well worth the trouble.

I wrote this play in 1952 for the Hiram College company of the Showboat *Majestic*, then touring the Ohio River and its tributaries. We had a lot of fun with it. Other companies have had fun with it since then. Those who have acted in "Lust" will notice few changes. I could, of course, have changed more, but so many people have acted in it, and have grown to love it, even for its many awkward moments, that I did not feel that I had the right to "improve" its language. Accordingly, I have made only some additions, chiefly an added first scene to introduce the audience to the idea of hissing the villain and cheering the hero.

I wrote *Piece of Work* in 1998. It runs about 100 minutes, takes a single unit set, contemporary costumes, no special effects beyond off-stage music and sound, three men and two women, no front curtain. It is included here partly to make a text long enough to interest a publisher, and partly because it's funny.—Brad Field

Lust, Lucre, & Liquor or Virtue Unbesmirched
▼

A Moral Representation In Fifteen Scenes And Five Acts Salubrious for the Entire Family Guaranteed to bring never a blush to the Modest Cheek

by
Brad Field

©1952; ® 1980

Costumes

Angeline Lovely: Blue, floor-length frock, bonnet for exteriors.

Mr. Lovely: Dark frock coat and matching pants, white shirt, black string tie; top hat for exteriors.

Mrs. Lovely: Dark, floor-length frock, apron.

Charles Lovely: Light frock-coat, contrasting pants, colored shirt contrasting coat, and a top hat, which he is constantly tipping, putting off, putting on.

Archibald Bullfinch: Black cape with a red lining, white shirt, black pants, black bow-tie, grey spats, grey gloves, dark vest, black top hat worn indoors and out, black mustache prominently painted.

Herman: Loose shirt in a "natural" color, brown pants or knickers in dark material, heavy shoes, knife in belt, no hat, no coat.

Smudge, Bartender, Engineer, Banker, all doubled by the same actor: blue pants, white shirt for all of them; Smudge as a station agent adds a blue coat and a blue cap; as a highwayman, neither, but adds a bandana; Bartender wears a clip-on mustache and a fright wig, a vest, but no coat; Engineer wears the kind of white beard and mustache that hook over the ears like spectacles, and the blue coat and cap; Banker wears a smooth wig, large black spectacles.

Dramatis Personsae

For the program:

LUST, LUCRE, and LIQUOR

by

Brad Field

Archibald Bullfinch, a villain of hideous depravity
Charles Lovely, a victim of intellectual and moral torpidity
Mr. Lovely, his father
Mrs. Lovely, his mother
Angeline Lovely, his sister
Herman, a woodsman, her inamorato
Smudge, a station agent and a road agent
Flob, a banker
A bartender

The Place, England, more or less.

The Time: A few days some time in 1850 to 1910.

Ladies annoyed–against their will–by men in the auditorium may apply to the Management for the appropriate forms on which to report the outrage.

Act I

▼

Scene 1: The railroad station, the "woods" drop upstage, with the edge of a shed appearing at stage right, with sign, "Dismal Seepage Station."

(AT RISE, enter SMUDGE right, with two suitcases.)

SMUDGE
I'm weary! Weary of lugging luggage! A station agent is supposed to play with the telegraph! Not supposed to boost bags and cart cases! Charles Lovely and his snobby friend just got off the train from the city, and they dump their junk on me!

(Crossing to stage left, to put the bags down.)

That mean man from the city that came here with Charles, he gives me ideas, you know what I mean?

(Enter CHARLES and BULLFINCH.)

SMUDGE (cont'd)
Ah, Mister Charles! It's good to see you back from the city.

CHARLES
Ah, Smudge, it's good to be back!

BULLFINCH
Egad, what a desert!

CHARLES
The trees, the bushes, the birds, the insects—

BULLFINCH
Insects! You never mentioned insects!

CHARLES
It's part of the charm of rural life, Archibald! Ah, Smudge, my friend from the city, Sir Archibald Bullfinch; Smudge, station agent here in Dismal Seepage.

SMUDGE
Pleased, I'm sure.

BULLFINCH
Are you indeed?

CHARLES
To be home again!

SMUDGE
I'm sure that they are all waiting up at Lovely Mansion to see you again.

BULLFINCH
Yeaaaahs! Up at Lovely Mansion! Your sister will be waiting, right?

CHARLES
Oh, oh! I am so transported with ecstasy, that, pardon me, I must pause for a moment of shallow breathing.

(CHARLES moves upstage.)

SMUDGE
'Scuse me.

BULLFINCH
I am not sure that you are excusable.

SMUDGE
I got a question, about the city.

BULLFINCH
(Aside) This bucolic familiarity is nauseous!

SMUDGE
See, I'm the station agent here in Dismal Seepage, and I spend a lot of time on the telegraph. The other station agents up and down the line—is it true what they say?

BULLFINCH
(Aside) This pest will tempt me soon to some imprudent expression of wrath!

SMUDGE
Do they bet on horses in the city?

BULLFINCH
What else are horses for?

SMUDGE
See, we have a few races among the farmers here-abouts, and wal...the truth is, there is some wagerin' on the sly. But according to what I hear on the telegraph, in the city you can bet thousands! Thousands!

BULLFINCH
Charles! Charles, let us be off. Off, I say!

SMUDGE
All I need it to raise a little money. I could get a bet down. I got a sure thing in the eighth at Belmont!

(CHARLES crosses to down stage again.)

CHARLES
Oh, Archibald, much though my being is engulfed with filial and fraternal passion at the prospect of seeing my family again...

(SMUDGE wanders to the left counting on his fingers.)

SMUDGE
(Sotto voce) Thousands! Thousands!

CHARLES
...there is—there is one thing I regret leaving behind in the city.

BULLFINCH
Aha, Charles, you miss the cards. Three no trump, doubled, vulnerable, fifty cents a point, and four two-way finesses to face!

CHARLES
Ah, no.

BULLFINCH
To win a hand like that is like stealing!

CHARLES
No, no.

BULLFINCH
No?

CHARLES
No.

BULLFINCH
Aha! Booze! Ginger ale and tequila with a dash of kerosene to spruce it up a bit!

CHARLES
Ah, no!

BULLFINCH
Chateauneuf de Pape and pretzels!

CHARLES
No, no!

BULLFINCH
No?

CHARLES
No. Worse than that. Worse, worse...

SMUDGE
If I could raise a little loot....

CHARLES
It shames me to confess it, Archibald, but the one pleasure that I regret leaving behind in the city—immoral thought I know it to be, a veritable pit of vice and corruption—something that fills me with nearly, pardon the expression, sexual lust—

BULLFINCH
Egad! Sounds fab!

CHARLES
It's cheering the hero and hissing the villain in the theatre! The theatre, that sink of vice and pollution!

BULLFINCH
Hissing the villain? How vulgar! Villains don't exist! And the theatre? That sink of tedium and insipidity?

CHARLES
Hissing the villain—I know it's wrong of me—but I miss it!

BULLFINCH
Can we finish with these aesthetic speculations and move on to green fields and pastures new?

(BULLFINCH conducts CHARLES OFF LEFT.)

BULLFINCH (CONT'D)
I long to browse amid your native glades and dells.

(EXIT LEFT CHARLES, BULLFINCH. RE-ENTER BULLFINCH, lungeing part-way on stage.)

BULLFINCH (Cont'd)
(Aside) And there to get a little nibble of his inimitable sister! Ha-ha!

(EXIT LEFT BULLFINCH.)

SMUDGE

That cussed critter with Charles gives me the willies and a good idea! I'll quit being a station agent and graduate to road agent! I'll get my grandpa's pistol off the mantelpiece and become a famous highwayman!

CURTAIN

ACT I, *Scene 2*: The Lovely mansion. Table center, two chairs left and right of it.

(AT RISE DISCOVER MR. LOVELY in stage left chair, MRS. LOVELY in stage right chair, ANGELINE standing stage left.)

ANGELINE

Oh, oh, father, I am scare able to contain myself over the return of my dear brother, Charles, from the city. Is he not overdue?

MR. LOVELY

Do not excite yourself, daughter. It is possible that the train was late.

MRS. LOVELY

Oh, heavens, yes!

ANGELINE
I do so wonder what his friend is like, the friend he is bringing home with him. He said in his letter, did he not, that he owed everything to this Sir Archibald Bullfinch?

MR. LOVELY
So he did, daughter.

(MR. LOVELY rises, crosses to center.)

MRS. LOVELY
Yes, indeed.

MR. LOVELY
This friend of Charles must be a kind and generous man to be such a help to our son.

MRS. LOVELY
Such a help.

MR. LOVELY
But a question impinges upon my brain.

ANGELINE
Yes, Father?

MR. LOVELY
In what manner did Charles need assistance? He never wrote to us that he was in any accident.

MRS. LOVELY

Never did.

MR. LOVELY

And we have trained never to become involved in the morass of squabbling that always accompanies sporting events or the world of entertainment. Perhaps this Bullfinch saved him from slanderous scandal.

ANGELINE

If that is the case, then this Archibald is indeed to be trusted as a true and dear friend.

MR. LOVELY

True, daughter. I have often affirmed that the finest thing one can do for a friend is to help him keep his name and reputation out of the mire of public discussion. Isn't that right, wife?

MRS. LOVELY

Oh, dear, yes.

(DOOR KNOCK OFF.)

ANGELINE

Someone knocks on the door!

(She crosses to right.)

That must be my dear brother Charles now!

(ENTER CHARLES RIGHT. MRS. LOVELY RISES.)

ANGELINE (CONT'D)

Brother!

CHARLES

Sister!

(Fervent handclasp. MRS. LOVELY crosses to CHARLES.)

MRS. LOVELY

Son!

CHARLES

Mother!

(Fervent handclasp. CHARLES crosses to MR. LOVELY.)

MR. LOVELY

Son!

CHARLES

Father!

(Fervent handclasp.)

Oh, what rapture, what unspeakable bliss, to be once more in the home of my childhood, amongst the family that loves me. But pardon in my ecstatic joy over my homecoming, I forgot my dear friend, who waits without. Won't you come in, Archibald.

(ENTER BULLFINCH RIGHT.)

CHARLES (CONT'D)
Dear family, I wish to introduce my dear friend, Sir Archibald Bullfinch. Archibald, my father, Mister Lovely.

MR. LOVELY
Welcome to Lovely Mansion, Sir Archibald.

BULLFINCH
(Bows) Thank you, Mister Lovely. I am proud to enter such a sumptuous (eyeing Angeline) and obviously refined abode.

CHARLES
And Mrs. Lovely, my mother.

BULLFINCH
I am charmed to make your acquaintance, Mrs. Lovely.

MRS. LOVELY
Oh, my yes.

CHARLES
And my dear sister, Angeline.

BULLFINCH
(Aside) Egan, the very girl whose portrait I saw in the city, in Charles' room! (Aloud) I am delighted to encounter such paragon of beauty so far from the metropolitan centers.

(EXIT LEFT MRS. LOVELY.)

BULLFINCH (CONT'D)
One sees so many of these maladroit maidens of equine form in the part of the country, that one hardly expects to find such a glorious flower in this patch of wretched weeds.

ANGELINE
Oh, Sir Archibald, you are too kind.

BULLFINCH
Come, come, we submerge ourselves in an ocean of formality. I insist that you address me simply as Archibald.

MR. LOVELY
I rejoice to see humbleness in a man of great station, Archibald.

(MR. LOVELY slaps him violently on the back.)

Greatly does it redound to your credit!

BULLFINCH
(Aside) Zounds, what a buffoon! (Aloud) Thank you, sir. I do my best.

(RE-ENTER MRS. LOVELY stage left.)

MR. LOVELY
And now if you are quite ready, Archibald, a hearty repast awaits us in the next room.

MRS. LOVELY
A hearty repast awaits us in the next room.

MR. LOVELY
Yes, wife.

(ANGELINE crosses to take the arm of MR. LOVELY, EXIT stage left.)

CHARLES
A hearty repast awaits us. Come Archibald I do entreat.

(EXIT CHARLES, MRS LOVELY stage left.)

BULLFINCH
Oh, what a glorious creature is that Angeline! Amongst the city's wealth of varied feminine allure, never have I seen such jewel of fresh, unspoiled innocence. An imprudent but avid and frenzied crazing, the controlling fact of my character, throbs within me. I am determined to win her, no matter what the cost. Thanks to my unsavory reputation in the city, none but the lowest type of women deign consort with me. But here, where I am unknown, here will I execute my foul deeds. Whatever is required, my fortune, or all the low devices with which I am so familiar, all will I use to make Angeline mine!

CURTAIN

ACT I, *Scene 3*: A wood.

(AT RISE, ENTER HERMAN.)

HERMAN
Here in the secret confines of this quiet wood, I await the arrival of my loved one, Angeline Lovely, the solitary object of my abject devotion. Though she be liberally endowed by nature with all the physical charms, these are not what enthrall my heart. Rather her unwavering aspect of piety, devotion, and noble sentiment. A purer and more virtuous girl is not to be found.

(FOOSTEPS OFF.)

Hark, an approaching footstep! But it is not hers. I would not have others see me in our accustomed trysting place.

(EXIT HERMAN. ENTER RIGHT, MR. LOVELY.)

MR. LOVELY
It is quiet and private here. (Calls off stage right) Oh, Angeline.

(ENTER RIGHT, ANGELINE.)

ANGELINE
Yes, Father?

MR. LOVELY
Come girl, I would speak with you in private, on a most important matter.

ANGELINE
But I thought we were going berry-picking!

MR. LOVELY
A mere ruse to gain a moment in private with you.

(ENTER HERMAN.)

HERMAN
Ah, there is my loved one now! But hold, her father is with her! I must hide!

(EXIT HERMAN.)

ANGELINE
What is it, Father?

MR. LOVELY
It concerns your future, my child. As you may know, the financial fortunes of the house of Lovely are not at their highest at this moment. To be brutally blunt, daughter, and do not at present tell your mother of this, the abyss of financial disaster yawns before Lovely Mansion.

ANGELINE
But Father, you have always taught me that care and concern over the problems of worldly wealth was vile and undignified.

MR. LOVELY
Quite so, my dear. And I have a plan in mind that relieve us of the necessity of stooping so low. I have just enough money left to provide you with quite a respectable dowry. 'Tis not a fortune, but 'tis enough, 'twill do. Is there not a man of some respectable means, with whom you could form a congenial union?

ANGELINE
You're referring to Squire Gasaway!

MR. LOVELY
Nonsense! The man is dangerous radical! He advocates paper money!

ANGELINE
And surely you don't mean Master Gumbottom!

MR. LOVELY
Certainly not! I'll confess, he is young, possessed of a large parcel of property, but he's unscrupulous scoundrel. He cheats at bridge!

ANGELINE
Horrors!

MR. LOVELY
Precisely!

ANGELINE
But Father, I cannot conceive of anyone else.

MR. LOVELY
Ah, but there is yet another!

ANGELINE
No!

MR. LOVELY
Yes! None other than Archibald Bullfinch!

(HERMAN sticks his head out from behind the Act Curtain)

HERMAN
Archibald! Great Scott, what is this?

(HERMAN withdraws.)

MR. LOVELY
Archibald is rich, good looking, and he has a sincere affection for you.

ANGELINE
Really?

MR. LOVELY
Really. I could tell by the multifarious small attentions which he has paid you.

ANGELINE
Dear Father, I fear that this requires some extensive cogitation. Hence, that I may be left in solitude to ponder this fateful step.

MR. LOVELY

I go! But think on this matter! Remember, we must preserve the honor of the Lovely name.

(EXIT MR. LOVELY.)

ANGELINE

Oh, dear, what to do?

(ENTER HERMAN.)

HERMAN

Angeline!

ANGELINE

Herman!

(Fervent handclasp.)

Oh, Herman, it is so wonderful to see you again, to gaze into your shining face, to peer into those eyes once more. When I am without you, I think ever of your splended eyes!

HERMAN

Ah, Angeline, it is not my eyes that are beautiful, but yours! So round, and how shall I express it? There are two of them! I cannot sleep at night but that the thought of them intrudes upon every dream.

ANGELINE

Herman, you are the most noble, most virtuous person that ever was born. You have an imperishably beautiful soul.

HERMAN
Ah, but your soul is more beautiful than mine!

ANGELINE
But Herman, your soul is pristine pure!

HERMAN
Say not so! Your soul is by far the more shining.

ANGELINE
But Herman, your soul is absolutely without blemish. You live in the woods, alone, where the contacts of those less cleaned-spirited attitudes cannot dirty it.

HERMAN
I insist, your soul is the more beautiful. for you live among the contagion and contamination of civilization, and yet remain a constant inspiration of purity to me.

ANGELINE
No, no, Herman, your soul is purer and more beautiful!

HERMAN
No, I beg to differ! Your sould is purer and more beautiful than mine!

ANGELINE
Yours is!

HERMAN
Yours is!

                    ANGELINE
Oh, mercy!

                    HERMAN
What?

                    ANGELINE
We are quarreling!

                    HERMAN
No!

                    ANGELINE
We must not!

                    HERMAN
Oh, dearest, never again!

                    ANGELINE
I pledge myself forever, never to quarrel with you again, Herman!

                    HERMAN
I too, pledge myself to the same, because, dearest one, you are always right.

                    ANGELINE
No, Herman, you are always right.

(ENTER SMUDGE with a bandanna over his nose, holding a huge pistol.)

HERMAN
Am not!

ANGELINE
Are so!

SMUDGE
Stick 'em up or I'll blow your brains out!

HERMAN
Smudge!

ANGELINE
Smudge! You nitwit!

HERMAN
Who is minding the telegraph down at the railroad station while you're out here in the woods?

ANGELINE
And what are you doing in that ridiculous get-up?

HERMAN
Be careful with that pistol!

ANGELINE
Does your mother know that you have taken that off her mantelpiece?

(SMUDGE pulls down the bandanna hiding his face.)

SMUDGE

Gee, don't tell my mother—

HERMAN

If you try to fire that thing, it will blow up in your face!

ANGELINE

I'm shocked! A grown man playing with his thing out in the woods!

SMUDGE

Gee, I'm sorry—

ANGELINE

Take that home and play with it there where it belongs! Silly man!

HERMAN

Half-wit!

SMUDGE

Gee, yeah, uh, good bye Angeline, Herman. (Aside) I don't command the respect I expect except from strangers. Better find one of those to rob.

(EXIT SMUDGE.)

ANGELINE

I thought he'd *never* leave!

HERMAN

Alone at last!

ANGELINE
Oh, Herman, why must we meet so secretly in the woods?

HERMAN
Your father's disapproval has forced us to this extreme. It grieves me deeply to behave like a skulking dog, but it your father's disapprobation continues, we too will have to continue thus.

ANGELINE
Father is too stubborn to believe that I could love anyone beneath my station.

HERMAN
It is agony to admit it, Angeline dear, but your father is right! That I, a poor woodsman, should think of marrying the daughter of the house of Lovely is surely unthinkable!

ANGELINE
Father told me to marry this Archibald Bullfinch. He's a noble man who is visiting our house. My brother Charles says that he owes everything to Archibald. Father says that I should be more receptive to Archibald's kindness, for 'pon my word, he does seem to find my company more than amenable.

HERMAN
And why should he not? But your father is, as I said, correct in his judgement. This noble man is obviously—Are you sure his first name is Archibald?

ANGELINE

I am positive. Why?

HERMAN

Oh, nothing, just that...well, anyway, this noble man is obviously the only person who is worthy of you. I am only a poor woodsman who cannot—are you sure that the last name was Bullfinch?

ANGELINE

Certainly!

HERMAN

Hm, well, yes. I am only a poor woodsman who cannot support you in the style to which you are accustomed. You must, for your family's sake and for your own, return home and to Archibald, and when he asks for you hand, give it to him freely, for no other deserves it! (Aside) Oh, agony! But it for her sake that I say it!

ANGELINE

Herman, you must be ill. Otherwise you could not say such a thing!

HERMAN

Go, Angeline! My brain reels!

ANGELINE

I will come back tomorrow when you are feeling better!

HERMAN

Nay, do not return! Go to Archibald and stay with him!

(EXIT ANGELINE.)

HERMAN (CONT'D)

She goes. She is gone! A secret burns within my bowels, but I shall never reveal it. To think that Lovely Mansion is on the brink of financial disaster, it passes all credibility. And then there is the matter of Archibald, about which I am pledged to hold my tongue. To think that Archibald should come back into my life now! Oh, cruel fate! For he is my foster brother, to whom I swore to abrogate my rightful inheritance, if he did not reveal to the discussion of the common throng a wretched scandal in which my father, his foster-parent, was involved. Archibald was a wild young man of sensuous tastes when I saw him last, but it would be a far better thing for Angeline to marry a man of substance and wealth like Archibald, rather than form a disgraceful union with me, merely a poor woodsman.

CURTAIN

Act II

Scene 1: Lovely Mansion. Table center, chairs left and right.

(AT RISE, ENTER BULLFINCH.)

BULLFINCH
Where, oh, where is that lass? I have searched the house high and low, but cannot find her. The place is empty. If she were here now, I could begin my design upon her without interruption. Egad, I am consumed with lust, my being seethes with flames!

(ENTER ANGELINE.)

BULLFINCH (CONT'D)
(Aside) Here she is now! I will ply her with words of seduction at once. (Aloud) Ah, Angeline, my rustic beauty, you are indeed ravishing today.

ANGELINE
Oh, good day, Archibald.

BULLFINCH
How now? Why so glum?

ANGELINE
I am in love with a young man of whom my father disapproves because he is naught but a lowly woodsman.

BULLFINCH
(Aside) What's this? Methinks I have competition for her favor! (Aloud) And rightly so, for who are you to question your father's decisions? He knows best. To marry a woodsman, a person far below your station, would bring a blot on the name and reputation of the house of Lovely. But I, my exquisite country maid, I am quite willing to put up with your quaint ways, and your station below my elevation, in the face of your overwhelming attraction for me. I am rich. I am the last of the Bullfinch line. Or soon will be. I need not worry over such trifles as a reputation.

(ANGELINE has been keeping the table and chairs between them.)

ANGELINE
No, Archibald. I love another.

BULLFINCH

(Aside) What's this? She refuses me? (Aloud) Come girl, enough of this shilly-shally and piffle. I offer you my love, access to the considerable Bullfinch fortune, my hand in marriage! (Aside) Egad, she drives me to extremes! (Aloud) Come a little closer, gal! You need not fear me!

ANGELINE

No, please, Archibald.

BULLFINCH

What do you mean, "please?" We are wasting time!

(BULLFINCH steps on one chair, on the table, on the other chair and pounces on her.)

Come now, a kiss!

(ENTER CHARLES.)

ANGELINE

No, Archibald! This is madness!

BULLFINCH

I warn you gal! Don't cross Archibald Bullfinch.

(CHARLES separates them.)

CHARLES

What is this? What do I see?

BULLFINCH
(Aside) Curses! Foiled!

CHARLES
Sir! Your behavior is heinous! You were born to high station and were presumably educated in the manners of a gentleman, a training that does not take exception to the tender sensitivities of the weaker sex. But now you act as if the fact that I owe you everything will excuse all manner of liberties taken with my dear sister!

BULLFINCH
I beg your forgiveness, Charles, and yours, Angeline. I was carried away by your beauty, lass, a beauty this is beyond compare, and allowed my emotions to override my better judgement.

CHARLES
Nevertheless, some sort of settlement must be made! Even if you cannot behave like gentleman toward women, perhaps you can face *me* like man! An invitation to meet me with your seconds at dawn tomorrow—

ANGELINE
Cease, Charles! This must not be! Sir Archibald is a guest in our domicile, and we must acts as hosts, with graciousness and decorum. You are forgiven, Archibald, but henceforth you must endeavor to control yourself. Come Charles.

(EXIT ANGELINE.)

CHARLES
Very well, but remember, Archibald. Keep a little *cooler* in the future.

(EXIT CHARLES.)

BULLFINCH
Well, I talked my way out of that little mess. That fool, Charles, challenging *me* to a duel! He knows I could kill him in an instant with either sword or pistol. Foiled, but merely by circumstance. Next time I shall arrange the circumstances to suit myself. I shall not give up, but continue in my foul campaign until I have conquered her scruples at last! To do that, I must first dispose of that cursed Charles. He will only get in my way again, unless he is taken care of. And I have the method! Ha-ha! It was only with the greatest of difficulty that Charles cured himself of the habit of overindulging in intoxicating liquors. The doctor in the city told him that should he ever again take too much, it would slowly but surely kill him. I will lure him to the local tavern. That will do the trick. Angeline will be alone then, and unprotected! I shall be able to do with her as I will!

CURTAIN

ACT II, *Scene 2*: The village common (just a repeat of the woods drop.)

(AT RISE, ENTER ANGELINE, ARCHIBALD, CHARLES.)

BULLFINCH
Did you enjoy the band concert?

ANGELINE
Oh, indeed, it was exceedingly fine.

CHARLES
Awfully decent of you to do this, after yesterday.

BULLFINCH
Pshaw! Forget it! 'Tis water under the bridge. (Aside) But water that has stained my memory with thoughts of revenge! (Aloud) The band concert was the least I do to atone for my loss of control. And now, after sitting in the heat of the afternoon, are we hot all a trifle parched?

ANGELINE
Why, that is a superb idea, Archibald. I am indeed thirsty, and would simply adore a cool glass of lemonade.

BULLFINCH
Then let us find a place to quench our thirsts. Tell me Charles, do I see truly. Is that not a tavern down the road?

CHARLES
(Sotto voce to Bullfinch) No, not the tavern! There must be some other place we can go. You know what happens to me in such a den.

BULLFINCH
Oh, piffle, just one won't hurt.

ANGELINE
I have never been inside a tavern before. That would be jolly.

BULLFINCH
See, your sister wants to go.

CHARLES
But sister, such places are usually so rough and crude.

ANGELINE
Oh, bosh!

(EXIT ANGELINE STAGE RIGHT.)

BULLFINCH
Oh, bosh, indeed! After all, has she not two strong men to protect her. And just one won't hurt you. Are you not a man!

CHARLES
Yes, I am a man! But to once more succumb to that vile liquid dispensed by yon poison shop would return me to the state of a beast! You were present when the physician warned me that should I again overindulge, I would suffer a lingering death!

BULLFINCH
Who spoke of overindulging? This will be just a quick one. First to satisfy your sister's curiosity, and second to wet our throats.

CHARLES
I still think I should stay away. You know, one drink leads to another. Ah, do you really think there's no harm in it?

BULLFINCH
(Aside) Aha! He weakens! (Aloud) Harm? Ridiculous!

CHARLES
Well, perhaps one little drink...(Speaks directly to audience) Do you really think I should?...They do say that alcohol kills slowly...But I'm in no hurry.

BULLFINCH
Hurry, Charles! Your sister is getting impatient!

(EXIT CHARLES, BULLFINCH STAGE RIGHT. RE-ENTER BULLFINCH, speaks directly to the audience.)

BULLFINCH
You may laugh, you jackals, but think on this! Have *you* any more will-power than that blob of jelly?

CURTAIN

ACT II, *Scene 3*: A tavern, bare essentials of which are back drop painted with rows of bottles on shelves; over them painted a framed portrait of a man's face; upstage right, a "bar," that is a piece of Masonite about four feet long, three feet high, painted to look like wood paneling; down stage left the table and two chairs.

(AT RISE DISCOVER BARTENDER BEHIND BAR. ENTER ANGELINE.)

ANGELINE
Oooh, ooh!

BARTENDER
Ooooh, oooh?

(ENTER CHARLES, BULLFINCH.)

BULLFINCH
Well, here we are. Observe, it's not so bad. A little on the crude side I will admit, and not the best appointed establishment that I have seen, but 'tis enough, 'twill serve.

ANGELINE
Oh, this is so sweet! How quaint and spoiled.

BARTENDER
Watch your language in here, Lady. This is a respectable dump. What'll it be?

BULLFINCH
Three doubles, on me!

ANGELINE
I'll have a lemonade, it you don't mind, Archibald.

BARTENDER
You'll have a what?

ANGELINE
A lemonade please.

(ANGELINE SITS IN STAGE LEFT CHAIR.)

BARTENDER
You got a big spender here, Sport.

BULLFINCH
Two doubles and a lemonade, then.

CHARLES
Oh, I'll have a lemonade too.

BULLFINCH
Lemonade! (Aside) Curses! This is not going as I had planned. (Aloud) Surely you will join me in a double, will you not, Charles?

(BARTENDER serves lemondade to the table.)

CHARLES
Well, I shouldn't, not really...

BULLFINCH
Think of how long it has been since you had a really good shot!

(BULLFINCH pours a drink for CHARLES, keeps the bottle, re-fills Charles' glass ad lib throughout.)

CHARLES
Oh, very well. (Drinks) Ugh! Not the best quality stuff, is it?

BULLFINCH
But invigorating!

CHARLES
Oh, yes, invigorating...

ANGELINE
The lemonade was good. But it was in such a small glass. I do believe I would like another.

(BARTENDER brings the bottle to the table.)

BULLFINCH
That's the spirit!

CHARLES
I feel better already!

BULLFINCH
Then let us have another!

CHARLES
No! Remember, you said that—

BULLFINCH
That two drinks will make you feel twice as good as one!

CHARLES
Well, I guess there is some logic in that...(Drinks)

(CHARLES sits in right chair.)

Goodness, I seem to be getting a little dizzy...

BULLFINCH
Well, you know the cure for that!

CHARLES
What's that?

BULLFINCH
Why, another drink, of course!

CHARLES
You don' say...

BULLFINCH
It will send waves of energy coursing through your veins. I revives the weary and calms the ill.

CHARLES
Thas' nice...Gimme a lil' drink. Ya know, Angeline, good ol' Arshbobble took good care o' me inna city. I dunno what I woulda' done 'thout good ol' Arshbobble. Whenever your brother got in trouble, there was good ol' Arshbobble, onna spot.

(CHARLES rises, crosses to the bar.)

CHARLES (CONT'D)
Poor ol' Charlie, he never got anywhere 'thout ol' Arsh.

BULLFINCH
Nothing that any person with the right sort of background wouldn't do.

CHARLES
Now, Arsh, les' not be shy and retirin'. Whup! Did you see that?

BULLFINCH
What?

(CHARLES points at the portrait over the bar.)

CHARLES
That guy up there winked at me!

BULLFINCH
Oh, he's probably drunk and thinks he knows you.

CHARLES
I don't like his looks!

BULLFINCH
Looks a genial sort of chap to me.

CHARLES
I'd like to punch him inna nose!

BULLFINCH
Now, Charles, careful. Remember, your sister is here.

CHARLES
Ooooo, tha's righ'! Angeline, ya' know what?

ANGELINE
What, Charles?

CHARLES
I won't tell!

ANGELINE
Why, Charles! I never knew you go be so much fun! What has come over you?

CHARLES
Oooo, I got unetshplored depfs. Way down deep isside, I'm—I'm hollow!

BULLFINCH
I say, Charles, you are a card! (Aside) Egad, what a revolting exhibition!

CHARLES
Arsh! You know, I don' think these drinks are helpin' me a bit! I seem to be gettin' worse. I'm shleepy and dishy, an' the whole rooms goin' 'roun' and 'roun'. A most dishtreshin' shitzuation...

(CHARLES hands his drink to BULLFINCH, falls flat on the floor. ANGELINE rises and rushes to kneel by CHARLES.)

ANGELINE
Oh, oh, what has happened to my dear brother? He is unconscious!

BULLFINCH
It is an illness that he contracted in the city. I curse myself for not recognizing it sooner. Apparently he has had a relapse.

ANGELINE
Oh, heavens, we at home had no idea that he was even sick!

BULLFINCH
'Tis not a serious ailment, but can be dangerous if left unattended for long. A cure will be instantaneous, but only a trained physician can administer it. Come, let us rush to the doctor through the woods!

ANGELINE
Let us go then, and quickly.

(EXIT ANGELINE, BULLFINCH. BARTENDER crosses to CHARLES, starts to lift him.)

BARTENDER

C'mon, Buster, on your feet! But where will I put him? The back room is full.

CHARLES

Whazzis?

BARTENDER

Ah, he's awake. Here, stand up by yourself.

CHARLES

Oh, I don't feel so good. Where's Angeline? Where's Archibald?

BULLFINCH

Will you get out of here? Or do I have to—

CHARLES

Wait a minute! What happened to the two who were with me?

BARTENDER

Oh, they left. Said they was gonna—

CHARLES

What? Angeline again alone with that scoundrel? I do not trust that man! Who knows what lubricious designs he may upon my sister?

(CHARLES stops at EXIT to turn, point at the portrait.)

I'll take care of *you*, later!

CURTAIN

Act III

▼

Scene 1: A wood.

ENTER BULLFINCH and ANGELINE

                      BULLFINCH
What's your hurry, gal? We have plenty of time.

                      ANGELINE
But my brother is ill at the tavern. We must get a doctor quickly.

                      BULLFINCH
Oh, piffle, Charles is feeling no pain. Come, let us tarry a while.

                      ANGELINE
But I—-this is not the way to the doctor's house!

BULLFINCH

How do you know?

ANGELINE

I have been to the doctor's before!

BULLFINCH

But you have not been to the doctor's house from the tavern, true?

ANGELINE

True. 'Tis true.

BULLFINCH

Gad, I quite willing to put with your quaint ways and low station in the face of your overwhelming attraction for me.

ANGELINE

No, no, Archibald. I love another.

BULLFINCH

(Aside) What's this? She refuses me again? (Aloud) Come, girl, enough of this shilly-shally and piffle. I offer you the more than considerable Bullfinch fortune. Come a little closer, gal. You need not fear me.

ANGELINE

No, please, Archibald.

BULLFINCH

What do you mean, "please?" We are wasting time! Come, a kiss!

ANGELINE
No, Archibald, this is madness.

(ENTER HERMAN.)

BULLFINCH
I warn you, gal, don't cross Archibald Bullfinch!

(HERMAN crosses to them, separates them.)

HERMAN
What is this? What do I see? Hold sir! Cease your advances!

BULLFINCH
Curses! Foiled again!

ANGELINE
My love!

HERMAN
My love!

BULLFINCH
My Gawd!

HERMAN
Sir, your behavior is heinous. You were, from your looks, born to high station and were presumably bred and educated in the manners f a gentleman, a training that does not take exception to the tender sensitivities of the weaker sex. But now you act as if the fact that this girl was not born to nobility will excuse all manner of liberties with her.

BULLFINCH
I beg your forgiveness, sir. And yours, Angeline. But I was carried away by your beauty, lass, a beauty that is beyond compare, and allowed my emotions to override my better judgement.

ANGELINE
You are forgiven, Archibald, but henceforth, you *must* endeavor to control yourself.

(EXIT ANGELINE.)

HERMAN
Keep a little cooler in the future.

(EXIT HERMAN.)

BULLFINCH
Well, I talked my way out of that little mess. Bah, thus again I am foiled by circumstance. But the next time, I shall arrange the circumstances to suit myself. I shall not give up, but continue in my foul campaign until I have conquered her scruples at last.

(ENTER SMUDGE, with bandanna on his face, holding pistol.)

BULLFINCH (CONT'D)
But first to dispose of that interfering bumpkin, whoever he was. What to do?

                    SMUDGE
Stick 'em up!

                    BULLFINCH
And *what* are you?

                    SMUDGE
I'm Smudge the notorious road agent. Stick 'em up!

                    BULLFINCH
And what is that rusted piece of junk that you hold in your hand?

                    SMUDGE
That's my pistol. If you don't stick 'em up, I'll shoot you!

                    BULLFINCH
I don't think that archaic piece will fire.

                    SMUDGE
Oh, yes it will!

    (SMUDGE clicks the pistol fruitlessly several times.)

                    SMUDGE (CONT'D)
Hmmm, I guess it won't.

                    BULLFINCH
Did you remember to load it?

                    SMUDGE
What kind of a fool do you think I am? Certainly I loaded it.

BULLFINCH
Where?

SMUDGE
Right there! See?

(BULLFINCH snatches the pistol.)

BULLFINCH
Aha! See, I have *you* in *my* power now!

(SMUDGE drops to his knees.)

SMUDGE
Please, mister, please don't shoot me. I have a wife and six starving kids.

BULLFINCH
You have *what*?

SMUDGE
I have a wife and *four* starving kids?

BULLFINCH
What?

SMUDGE
I got a sure thing in the eighth at Belmont.

BULLFINCH
That's more like it. How would you like to earn a two-spot?

SMUDGE

Do I have to work?

BULLFINCH

You just have to help me. Do you know a woodsman who lives near here?

SMUDGE

I don't know him and he doesn't know me. But I know where he lives.

BULLFINCH

Where?

SMUDGE

Gimme the two-spot, and I'll tell you.

(BULLFINCH threatens with the pistol.)

BULLFINCH

Where does he live?

SMUDGE

Up the road and over the hill and down by the railroad tracks.

(ENTER CHARLES.)

CHARLES

Oh, I am so ill! I wish I were dead!

BULLFINCH
You say this woodsman lives by the railroad tracks.

SMUDGE
Right by 'em.

CHARLES
What is this? Archibald in conversation with Smudge? I'll hide and listen!

(EXIT CHARLES.)

BULLFINCH
I should be very happy if this inconvenient woodsman should happen to have an accident.

SMUDGE
Happy accident.

BULLFINCH
You and I, with a little ingenuity, can perhaps arrange such an accident.

SMUDGE
Arranged accident.

BULLFINCH
Living so near the railroad, his early demise would be no surprise, would it, if he were run over by the express? Very natural, what?

SMUDGE

Natural accident.

BULLFINCH

Smudge, we have work to do!

SMUDGE

Work? Surely you jest!

BULLFINCH

Come, Smudge!

(EXIT, BULLFINCH, SMUDGE. ENTER CHARLES.)

CHARLES

Bt the Grear Horned Spoon! Rascality runs amuck! What is there to do? I am deathly ill. The doctor warned me that should I again overindulge, I would surely perish. The vile curse of liquor quite o'erwhelms my spirit! My bowels decay within me!

(Produces a hot water bottle from beneath his shirt.)

Great Zeus! One kidney gone!

CURTAIN

ACT III, *Scene 2*: Lovely Mansion.

(AT RISE, DISCOVER ANGELINE.)

ANGELINE

Oh, woe, oh, woe is me! Methinks I am losing Herman's steadfast affection. All the way back to the house, he spoke not a word, but seemed lost in thought. I love dear Herman so. He has such a beautiful soul. Father says that I should marry Archibald to repair the fortunes of the house of Lovely. Archibald is rich and handsome, with a noble station. It would be jolly to live in a big house with many servants. But I am true to Herman. I cannot marry Archibald. Yet somehow Lovely Mansion must be saved. How else can we do it than I marry Archibald? I am confused. But who is this I see coming?

(ENTER CHARLES.)

ANGELINE (CONT'D)

'This Charles, and he is conscious again!

CHARLES

Oh, my dearest sister, something terrible has come to pass.

ANGELINE

What are you saying?

CHARLES

'Tis Archibald.

ANGELINE

Archibald?

CHARLES

Do not marry him, Angeline. He is a rogue, a noble, but a rogue, and, if you will pardon the expression, a cad!

ANGELINE

Heavens!

CHARLES

Do you remember a statement I made, when I introduced him to the family? I said then that I owed Archibald everything. Well, I meant it. But I didn't mean my honor, or my life, but my money!

ANGELINE

Money? How vulgar!

CHARLES

True, too true. While in the city I gambled and lost. My hand at cards is not the most skilled ever witnessed. But I still have my suspicions concerning my opponents. Suffice it to say, I borrowed money from Archibald in an attempt to recoup my losses. But I lost all that too. I borrowed more money than I could ever hope to repay. Now I have given him every coin I own, and he forces me to bring him into my own home on the threat that he will reveal all and drag the whole matter into court.

ANGELINE

This transcends all belief!

CHARLES
But that is not all. The worst I have yet to divulge.

ANGELINE
What? What?

CHARLES
On my way home from the tavern, I happened upon Archibald in conversation with that scoundrel Smudge.

ANGELINE
What means this?

CHARLES
I heard them plotting together. To plot some foul deed on the person of a local woodsman.

ANGELINE
Oh, dear, it is against Herman, my love, that they plot.

CHARLES
What were they going to do? Something awful. Can't remember what it was. But it was awful. Excuse me, sister, I am not well. I must retire to other quarters! My innards disintegrate! Great Caesar's ghost!

(CHARLES produces from under his shirt an inflated balloon, which he lets go to fly farting across the stage.)

My liver!

(EXIT CHARLES.)

ANGELINE

Oh, dear, dear, what am I to do? I am only a poor delicate girl. What am I against the strength of Archibald and Smudge? I tremble with fear! But Herman, my own true love, is in danger! Trepidation engulfs me! But I must do something. I will fly as fast as my feet can carry me to Herman's woodland cabin!

EXIT at

CURTAIN

ACT III, *Scene 3*: A wood, with railroad tracks in the foreground. Tracks may consist of a flat about a foot and half wide, and as long as the width of the stage, laid on its side and tipped back from the audience at about 45 degrees, with the tracks and ties painted it in perspective.

(ENTER BULLFINCH, SMUDGE.)

BULLFINCH

Aha! We have beaten that accursed woodsman here. Now nothing remains but to wait for him. How long before the next train?

SMUDGE

Maybe ten minutes or so.

BULLFINCH

Where can I hide while you talk to that woodsman?

SMUDGE

Try the sawmill over behind those trees.

(SMUDGE points up left.)

BULLFINCH

Fine. Now, remember what I told you-whup! Here comes to the woodsman now. Caution, caution!

(EXIT BULLFINCH up left. ENTER HERMAN down left.)

HERMAN

Good day, my good man. What can I do for you?

SMUDGE

Tell me, how long can I keep a fire burning with a bundle of wood this size?

(SMUDGE holds up his hands two feet apart. HERMAN imitates his gesture.)

HERMAN

This size? Oh, about an afternoon, I should judge.

(ENTER BULLFINCH up left, holding a piece of rope, behind HERMAN.)

SMUDGE
How long would a load of wood this big last?

*(SMUDGE stretches his arms wide.
HERMAN imitates his gesture.)*

HERMAN
About an afternoon and an evening, I figure.

SMUDGE
How about a load of wood this big?

*(SMUDGE stretches arms clear around behind himself.
HERMAN imitates his gesture.)*

HERMAN
This big? Why, I suppose—

BULLFINCH
Aha!

*(BULLFINCH loops his piece of rope around Herman's
back-stretched hands.)*

HERMAN
What occurs!

BULLFINCH
Get him tied!

*(SMUDGE pulls a piece of rope from his pocket and ties
Herman's ankles.)*

HERMAN
What means this vile assault?

SMUDGE
I got his legs!

HERMAN
Help! Assassins!

BULLFINCH
Dump him across the track here!

(They put him in a sitting position, his feet downstage, his back against the "tracks.")

HERMAN
This is unmannerly behavior! It lacks couth!

BULLFINCH
Gag him!

(SMUDGE shoves handkerchief in Herman's mouth.)

SMUDGE
The train should be along soon!

BULLFINCH
Very soon indeed! Now, bumpkin, now you see the penalty for crossing Archibald Bullfinch! Interrupt my wooing, eh? Compete against me for the hand of Angeline Lovely, eh? Now you shall suffer for your mistake. Think on that train coming, rumbling down the track straight for the neck that supports that fat head of yours!

SMUDGE
Excuse me, but the conductor on this train knows me, and if he saw us together, he'd report it!

BULLFINCH
Very well, we shall retire to the sawmill until the train has passed. But I do so like to gloat!

(EXIT SMUDGE up left.)

BULLFINCH (CONT'D)
Goodbye, oaf. But don't be sad! Remember the price you'll bring on the market as ground round steak. Ha-ha-ha!

*(EXIT BULLFINCH up left.
ENTER ANGELINE up right.)*

ANGELINE
Oh, dear, what is this? My true love, Herman, tied to the railroad tracks.

(SOUND OFF: Train whistle.)

ANGELINE (CONT'D)
What to do? I must try the knots!

(SOUND OFF: Train whistle.)

They are so hard! Aha, the knife in his belt!

> *(SOUND OFF: Train whistle three times.
> ANGELINE "cuts" the rope on Herman's hands.)*

There, free, saved, victory!

HERMAN, ANGELINE lunge away from the tracks to fall along the foot lights.
A large Masonite cut-out of a train, painted to look like a cartoon caricature of an ancient wood-burner, about eight feet long and four feet high, with the ENGINEER, holding it up, while sticking his face out of the cut-out window, runs as rapidly as the ENGINEER can sprint from off-stage left to off-stage right.

CURTAIN

This might be a good spot for an intermission or an entr'act to cover the time needed for set change for the next scene.

Act IV

▼

Scene 1: Interior of a sawmill. The backdrop of a wooden wall, with saw down left. The saw could consist of a crude table eight feet by two feet, and circular saw-blade cut from beaver-board, the axle of which is fastened underneath to the stage-left end of the table. At the center-stage end of the table the players need a second two-eight, one end of which rests on the table, and the other slants to the floor. This slanted board needs an inconspicuous ridge at the bottom end where the heroine can rest her heels. A rope attached to the lower end of the board, and several lash-cleats along the sides of the board, with which the villain may quickly and smoothly tie up the heroine.

(AT RISE DISCOVER BULLFINCH, SMUDGE, peering toward off right.)

BULLFINCH
Did you hear what she called that woodsman?

SMUDGE
Yeah, Herman!

BULLFINCH
Herman! Can it be?

SMUDGE
That's his name.

BULLFINCH
Herman! I thought I was rid of that schnook! Something will have to be done about him!

(SMUDGE registers disgust. During this speech, he ducks under the back of Bullfinch's cape, then reappears with his wallet. EXIT SMUDGE right.)

BULLFINCH (CONT'D)
But what? By the terms of the contract that he made with me, I shall enjoy his fortune only until he dies. At that time, it will abrogate back to my foster cousin, Percy, who is, I assure you, a monumental ass! But there are other ways! Herman is, I suspect, passionately devoted to Angeline. If so, the removal of that girl from the scene would sunder his sanity! He is a sensitive creature; he would not be able to stand the blow to his intellect and emotions. Then he would be putty in my hands. I will drive him to Bedlam, there to be a spectacle of pity and ridicule to the multitudes. How, how to proceed? Smudge?

BULLFINCH (CONT'D)
Smudge, I have a little job for you for which I will pay—Smudge, where are you? Here, I'll give you that two-spot now...Where is the....gone! That rogue! Aha, but what do I see? Herman pursues Smudge through the woods! And Angeline comes *here* for sanctuary! *This* should be a simple matter!

(BULLFINCH retires behind the saw table. ENTER ANGELINE stage right. BULLFINCH steps forward.)

BULLFINCH
Aha, Angeline! We meet again!

ANGELINE
Archibald! You! Here!

BULLFINCH
Yes, Angeline! Cozy, isn't it?

ANGELINE
Stay away from me! Don't touch me! Charles has told me all about you! You are a rogue, a noble, but a rogue, and if you'll pardon the expression, a cad! I'm going home!

BULLFINCH
I beg to differ, Angeline! You are not going home! You are staying here! I am determined that if I cannot have you, no one shall.

(BULLFINCH pulls out the pistol.)

ANGELINE
What are you going to do? What is that?

BULLFINCH
That is a pistol, my dear.

ANGELINE
You are going to shoot me!

BULLFINCH
Why, Angeline, how could you say such a thing! (Aside) This pistol is old. 'Twould be dangerous to attempt to fire it. It might explode in my face. (Aloud) Nay, gal, I shall not shoot you.

(BULLFINCH puts pistol back into his belt.)

I do not propose to leave your body in all its radiant beauty on the scene for Herman to find and to mourn over. Nay, I will leave only the mutilated and butchered remains!

(BULLFINCH seizes her and wrestles her to the right, leans her back on the slanted board.)

ANGELINE
Leave off your grasp, villain!

BULLFINCH
Come, come, gal! It will all be over in a minute!

(BULLFINCH lashes her legs and waist.)

ANGELINE
You beast! This is monstrous!

BULLFINCH
Do not be difficult!

ANGELINE
Oh, please, I beg you not to do this!

BULLFINCH
Aha! Will you marry me, then?

ANGELINE
Never! Death and mutilation before that!

BULLFINCH
As you wish it, gal!

(BULLFINCH finishes tying her arms. Turns on the saw with a lever that will also be convenient to the hero who is to enter in a few lines.
SOUND OFF: Screaming buzz-saw on tape, or a large pair of band cymbals rubbed together.
BULLFINCH lifts the lower end of the slanted board and slides it slowly toward saw at the other end.)

ANGELINE
Help! Help! Murder! Assassin! Stop, please, stop! Oh, save me, someone, save me!

(ENTER HERMAN right.)

####### HERMAN
I'll save you, dear one!

(HERMAN grabs BULLFINCH. They struggle, each holding the other's lapels.
HERMAN swings a blow.
BULLFINCH reacts as if hit, staggers OFF RIGHT.
HERMAN switches off the saw.
SOUND: Saw noise stops.)

####### ANGELINE
Oh, Herman, you have saved me!

####### HERMAN
Now we're even!

CURTAIN

ACT IV, *Scene 2*: Lovely Mansion.

(AT RISE, DISCOVER MR. LOVELY, MRS. LOVELY, CHARLES, ANGELINE.)

####### ANGELINE
'Tis time you told Father all, Charles.

CHARLES
True, but I fear that he will drive me from his house when he hears of my disgraceful behavior in the city.

ANGELINE
Let me speak to him first. Father? I have just made a horrible discovery!

MR. LOVELY
What?

MRS. LOVELY
What, what?

ANGELINE
'Tis about Archibald.

MR. LOVELY
Our dear and trusted friend, Archibald? I won't hear a word said against him.

MRS. LOVELY
Certainly not!

ANGELINE
But you must!

MRS. LOVELY
Yes, indeed!

ANGELINE
He has just tried to murder me!

MR. LOVELY

What?

MRS. LOVELY

Well, bless my soul!

ANGELINE

He tried to cut me up on the sawmill. It was only Herman who saved me.

MR. LOVELY

Have you been seeing that loafer again?

MRS. LOVELY

Shame on you!

ANGELINE

What have I said?

CHARLES

Father, I have a horrible confession to make.

MR. LOVELY

Now what?

CHARLES

When I went to the city, I made a wretched mistake, forgot your excellent advice, and fell in with evil men. We played bridge for money. I lost, lost quite extensively.

MR. LOVELY
But Archibald rescued you.

CHARLES
Far from it. He was the worst of the lot. When I lost to him and to his cohorts, I borrowed money from him in an attempt to recoup my losses. But I lost all that too. And I signed papers demanding more money than I can pay.

MR. LOVELY
Bah! I don't believe it!

CHARLES
But it's true!

MR. LOVELY
Nonsense! A noble, handsome man like Archibald, a gambler?

CHARLES
No, no gamble at all. He cheats!

ENTER BULLFINCH.

MR. LOVELY
Archibald, cheat at bridge? That's a very serious accusation, Charles.

(ENTER BULLFINCH right.)

CHARLES
Here's the villain now

BULLFINCH
Aha, found you at last, Charles. I have decided that I can wait no longer for the debt that you owe.

CHARLES
You know I don't have the money.

BULLFINCH
I want that debt paid at once! Three thousand, one the line.

CHARLES
But I've given you every coin I have. I have nothing left!

MR. LOVELY
Then it's true? Three thousand?

BULLFINCH
Charles, you must pay that debt by tomorrow, or else!

CHARLES
Or else what? If I haven't got it, I haven't got it.

BULLFINCH
Or else I will take the case to court!

MR. LOVELY
And risk the reputation of the house of Lovely by sordid public recriminations? Never! Come back tomorrow and you shall have your filthy lucre. But now, now that the scales have fallen from my eyes, I can see you as you really are, a mean despicable cheat at bridge. I cannot stand the sight of you! Get out of my house!

(MR. LOVELY grabs BULLFINCH by the lapels, throws him up right.)

BULLFINCH
I shall expect the money by tomorrow, or I will take the case to court!

(EXIT BULLFINCH. RE-ENTER BULLFINCH.)

BULLFINCH
No fudging about, now!

MR. LOVELY
Out!

CHARLES
Out!

MRS. LOVELY
Out!

BULLFINCH
Ha-ha-hah!

(EXIT BULLFINCH.)

CHARLES
How can you pay the debt, Father? Lovely Mansion itself is on the brink of financial disaster.

MRS. LOVELY

Surely not!

MR. LOVELY

You have been talking with your sister!

ANGELINE

True, Father.

MR. LOVELY

There is only one way.

ANGELINE

Yes, Father?

MR. LOVELY

Yes, Daughter.

ANGELINE

What, Father?

MR. LOVELY

Lovely Mansion. I must mortgage it with Banker Flob.

CHARLES

Not that!

ANGELINE

How wretched!

MRS. LOVELY

Fearful!

MR. LOVELY
'Tis a far, far better thing to indulge in the relative privacy of crass commercialism than to allow the disgrace of public legal entanglement to blot the family escutcheon.

CHARLES
Father, forgive me for being the cause of all this misery and despair.

MR. LOVELY
Nay, squandering prodigal, I cannot! You have estranged yourself from filial devotion. You have severed the bonds of family unity!

CHARLES
Say not so! Accept me once more into the fold of the family, in my humility and abject grief.

MR. LOVELY
Your tearful words cannot prevail. You have crossed the boundary of prudent behavior and nothing in this world can restore you.

ANGELINE
Oh, Father, it was but a momentary deviation from the path of discretion, and when we have mortgaged our beloved homestead, all will be well.

(CHARLES kneels by a chair.)

CHARLES

I will work and scrimp and save for the remainder of my life, if necessary, to pay back that three thousand.

(CHARLES slaps a hand for emphasis on the chair seat. MR. LOVELY sits on the seat. CHARLES spends the rest of the speech trying to extract his hand.)

MR. LOVELY

Very well, I relent. But you must never forget what you have caused, and more than likely because you insisted on leading from kings, and seldom, if ever drew trump. Many a man is walking the streets of the city, homeless, heartbroken, and miserable with cold and fatigue, because he failed to draw his trump. Now I must leave.

*(MR. LOVELY rises.
CHARLES nurses his hand.)*

MR. LOVELY (CONT'D)

I am on my way to visit Banker Flob.

*(EXIT MR. LOVELY.
BULLFINCH thrusts his head on stage.)*

BULLFINCH

(Aside) Aha! I have heard it all! I will follow! I've got them now! Ha-hah!

CURTAIN

ACT IV, *Scene 3*: A bank. A plain drop with a table, chair.

(AT RISE, DISCOVER BANKER FLOB. ENTER MR. LOVELY.)

MR. LOVELY
Good morrow to you, Banker Flob.

BANKER FLOB
Good morrow to *you*, Mr. Lovely. To what purpose may I attribute the occasion of this visit, hmmmm?

MR. LOVELY
It pains me deeply to say this, Banker, and I hope you will keep all the circumstance of this meeting *indiscetorium ad infinitum...*

BANKER FLOB
(Aside) This sounds juicy! (Aloud) Let us get to the meat of the matter, shall we, hmmm?

MR. LOVELY
To be brutally blunt about it, Banker, I need three thousand.

BANKER FLOB
Three thousand? Normally we bankers do not *give* money. We *take* it.

MR. LOVELY
I wish to mortgage Lovely Mansion for the three thousand.

BANKER FLOB
How now, Mr. Lovely! *You* mortgage Lovely Mansion?

MR. LOVELY
These are evil times, Banker, and the star of the fortunes of the house of Lovely is obscured by a malignant cloud, whose sulphurous fumes threaten to strangle all the hopes and dreams of the Lovely clan.

BANKER FLOB
Do tell! Well, three thousand is a great deal of money, Mr. Lovely, hmmmm?

MR. LOVELY
It is indeed, Banker. If it were less, I would not mortgage my home.

BANKER FLOB
I see! Well, I think that within the realm of alternatives that life offers us, there must be something to which we can turn.

(BANKER FLOB produces a document with red seals and ribbons.)

BANKER FLOB (CONT'D)
Sign here. And here. And here.

(BANKER FLOB pounds the document in six different places with a rubber stamp. Hands Mr. Lovely a piece of paper plainly labeled "CHECK.")

Here you are Mr. Lovely.

MR. LOVELY
Thank you, Banker Flob.

BANKER FLOB
Thank *you*, Mr. Lovely.

MR. LOVELY
Good day, Banker Flob.

BANKER FLOB
Good day, Mr. Lovely.

*(EXIT MR. LOVELY.
BANKER FLOB waggles ribboned document, blows on it,
to dry the ink.
ENTER BULFINCH.)*

BULLFINCH
Good day, Banker!

BANKER FLOB
Good day, sir. Can I help you?

BULLFINCH
Yes, you can. I need a mortgage.

BANKER FLOB
What do you wish to mortgage?

BULLFINCH
I don't wish to mortgage *anything*! I would purchase one.

BANKER FLOB
Oh? Which one, hmmmm?

BULLFINCH
I'm not particular, anyone will do. Here's one!

(BULFINCH snatches the ribboned paper from the banker's hands.)

BULLFINCH (CONT'D)
(reading) Blah-blah,blah-blah,
Blah-blah, blah-blah,
Blah-blah-blah?
Blah-blah,
Blah-blah
Blah-blah-blah!

Yes, a likely looking specimen. I'll give you six thousand for it.

BANKER FLOB
Six thousand! (Aside) Obviously demented! (Aloud) Done!

BULFINCH hands over a piece of paper clearly marked "CHECK."

BULLFINCH
How soon may I foreclose?

BANKER FLOB
In three months. Just a minute! I'll put the date on it.

BULLFINCH
Never mind! I can put the date in myself! Thank you, sir, and good day.

(EXIT BULLFINCH.)

BANKER FLOB
I have a feeling that something not quite right has happened here, but why complain if I've doubled my money in three minutes, hmmmm?

CURTAIN

Act V

Scene 1: The Lovely Mansion.

*(AT RISE DISCOVER MR. LOVELY, MRS. LOVELY, ANGELINE, CHARLES.
ENTER BULLFINCH.)*

BULLFINCH
Well, good morning, Mr. Lovely, good morning all! You have the three thousand, I presume, to pay the debt owed to me by your son, Charles?

MR. LOVELY
Yes, bounder, here it is. Now get out of my house!

BULLFINCH
I beg to differ, my driveling, doltish friend. **I** order *you* out of *my* house!

MR. LOVELY
What is the meaning of this outrage?

BULLFINCH
I have purchased the mortgage to Lovely Mansion, and I am now foreclosing. Unless you have an additional three thousand to pay off the mortgage, I would be pleased to have you all *off* the premises!

CHARLES
Oh the disgrace of it all, that I should be he cause of it! Oh, agony, oh soul-corroding anguish, the stench of my misdeeds contaminates the hearth and home that I love. I cannot stand it! I must fly!

(EXIT CHARLES.)

ANGELINE
Charles, come back! He's gone!

MR. LOVELY
What do you mean, foreclose? I have at least three months to pay off.

BULLFINCH
Aha, but as Angeline may well know, I am not a patient man. I could not wait. I bought the mortgage before that fool banker had a chance to put the date on it and set back the date to three months ago myself, so that it falls due *today*!

ANGELINE
You treacherous wretch, how could you stoop to such low tricks?

BULLFINCH
You'll have to prove that in court!

MR. LOVELY
In court! A trial! Oh, dishonor. How shameful!

MRS. LOVELY
It's so nasty!

BULLFINCH
Do I presume correctly when I say that you not have the additional three thousand?

MR. LOVELY
All is lost! We are undone!

BULLFINCH
Not so! There is yet an answer to all your problems.

MR. LOVELY
How now, what is this?

BULLFINCH
I will burn the mortgage before your very eyes upon you compliance with one small request.

ALL in chorus
Well?

BULLFINCH
The hand of Angeline Lovely in marriage!

ANGELINE
Oh, no!

MR. LOVELY
Never!

MRS. LOVELY
Enh-eh!

BULLFINCH
If you people must persist in this stubborn attitude, I shall be forced to pitch you all bodily into the street, where you shall wander, homeless, penniless vagrants, forever dishonored!

ANGELINE
Stop! Father! Mother! The family honor! It must be preserved! I will marry him!

MR. LOVELY
Never! I will not permit it! Union my marriage with the line of Bullfinch would be more dishonorable than poverty!

ANGELINE
Nay, poverty is worse! Remember the family name!

MR. LOVELY
I should die before I shall conjoin with the name of Lovely, the epithet of Bullfinch!

BULLFINCH
I beg your pardon, but since you cannot agree between the two of you, why do you not refer the decision to the razor-edged intellect of Mrs. Lovely?

MR. LOVELY
Yes, wife! Tell us! Which is worse?

ANGELINE
Poverty or Bullfinch?

MRS. LOVELY
Who, me?

CURTAIN

ACT V, *Scene 2*: A wood.

(ENTER CHARLES, right, pushed on my BARTENDER.)

BARTENDER
And keep out! I won't have my grandpa's portrait insulted!

(EXIT BARTENDER right.)

CHARLES

Oh, woe, misery! And utter abnegation, too! That is my lot. I couldn't stand to see what Archibald is doing to my family, and the bartender refuses me the only means I know for ignoring it: booze! Yet, booze, alas it is booze, not the lack of it, that gnaws at my inner being now! What pain, what suffering, what an intense sensation of internal vacuity! Aha, the banker!

(ENTER BANKER FLOB LEFT. This means that the actor of both this role and the Bartender has made a quick change while running across, back stage.)

BANKER FLOB

Aha, Charles!

CHARLES

Aha, that mortgage—

BANKER FLOB

Aha, business couldn't be better!

CHARLES

The date got changed—

BANKER FLOB

Aha! Made a wad on that one! Got it right here!

BANKER FLOB pats his pocket.

CHARLES

And Archibald is using it—

BANKER FLOB
Kind of hate to leave all that money lying around at the bank over night. Never can tell what might happen to it there!

CHARLES
But listen—

BANKER FLOB
How about a quickie?

CHARLES
What? Oh, sorry, no. I'm *boozer non grata* with that portrait—

BANKER FLOB
I thought I'd have one on the way home; celebrate. Isn't every day you double your money in three minutes!

CHARLES
But he's changing the date—

BANKER FLOB
See you 'round, Charlie!

(EXIT BANKER right.)

CHARLES
But wait! Wait! Egad, I envy him. I wish I could go in there and—No! No, I mustn't think of that now! I must concentrate, do something to save Lovely Mansion...But how? I

CHARLES

need help! Herman? Herman! That's it! Herman, Herman! Where are you? Oooh, yigga! My duodenum is like two pair of blue jeans, torn to very shreds!

(ENTER SMUDGE left. This means that the actor of both this role and the Banker Flob has made a quick change, during a running cross, back stage.)

SMUDGE

Stick 'em up!

CHARLES

What? Wrong man.

SMUDGE

Sorry, Charlie. All bent over like that, I hardly recognized you.

CHARLES

Try the banker.

SMUDGE

Yeah? Where is he?

CHARLES

In the bar. When the portrait gets through with him, he'll be right out.

SMUDGE

Oh, yeah? Good idea!

CHARLES

Smudge, can—

SMUDGE

Later, Charlie. Busy now.

(EXIT SMUDGE right.)

CHARLES

The only one left is Herman. Herman, where are you? Oh, I am sick, mortally ill. That one last drink sunders this mortal beast, sinew by sinew. I am dying from the insidious effects of alcohol. Oh, that I should have been the cause of such misfortune to the mother that bore me, the father that raised me, the sister who loved me. Ooops! (Produces a coil or a piece of hose from beneath his coat.)

There go my intestines! Oh, woe, misfortune!

(ENTER HERMAN.)

HERMAN

Charles!

CHARLES

Herman!

HERMAN

I heard you call. What is the matter?

CHARLES

All is awry. Woe, misfortune and folly!

HERMAN
Steady, boy! Now, what is this?

CHARLES
Archibald Bullfinch is foreclosing the mortgage on Lovely Mansion!

HERMAN
What?

CHARLES
Oh, I forgot to tell you. He is an evil man with whom I—

HERMAN
Never mind! How did he get a mortgage on Lovely Mansion?

CHARLES
He bought it from Banker Flob in order to—

HERMAN
How did Banker Flob get the mortgage?

CHARLES
Father mortgaged Lovely Mansion to get the three thousand.

HERMAN
But what did he need the three thousand for?

CHARLES
To pay the gambling debts that I owe to Archibald.

HERMAN
Gambling debts? *You* gamble?

CHARLES
'Twas vile, I know. But the weak of spirit can resist all but temptation. Now all is lost, and I am dying from the effects of that one last drink which Archibald pressed into my insatiable hands!

HERMAN
The time for silence is at an end! I must now reveal my long enshrouded secret to the world, to free the family of the one I love from this parasite!

CHARLES
But what is to be done?

HERMAN
There is always a way if you are *man* enough to follow it out!

CHARLES
So there is!

(CHARLES steals the knife from Herman's belt.)

HERMAN
Come! Let us be off to Lovely Mansion!

(EXIT HERMAN left. CHARLES raises the knife.)

CHARLES
I may die tonight, but I will drag another with me into the murky depths of Hell!

CURTAIN

ACT V, *Scene 3*: Lovely Mansion.

(AT RISE, DISCOVER MR. LOVELY, BULLFINCH, MRS. LOVELY, ANGELINE in exactly the same pose as at the curtain of Act V, scene 1.)

BULLFINCH
Well, woman?

MRS. LOVELY
Let me think!

MR. LOVELY
Come, come!

MRS. LOVELY
I cannot decide.

ANGELINE
Please, Mother!

MRS. LOVELY

It is so hard!

(ENTER HERMAN.)

HERMAN

Whoa! Halt! Stop! Cease! Desist! Subside! Ebb!

BULLFINCH

What is this?

HERMAN

It is I, heretofore known as Herman, the woodsman! But now I reveal my full name as Herman Bullfinch. I am Archibald's foster brother, and the rightful heir to our father's fortune!

BULLFINCH

But I am the last of the Bullfinch line!

HERMAN

How, now, Archibald! Do no say that you do not recognize me!

BULLFINCH

I recognize you, my oafish relation, but I am still the last of the Bullfinch line!

HERMAN

I beg to differ—

BULLFINCH

Excuse me! I should have said, I *will* be the last of the Bullfinch line.

(Draws the pistol from his belt.)
As soon as I pull the trigger on this pistol that is now aimed directly at your heart!

ANGELINE

You fiend!

MR. LOVELY

But tell me, Herman! Why are you now willing to reveal your name?

HERMAN

Because previously I had sworn to keep silent if Archibald would not reveal a scandal in which my father, his foster-parent, was embroiled. But now, in order to save the family of the one I love from the depredations of this denizen of iniquity, I have decided to let Archibald reveal all and to bear the shame myself!

BULLFINCH

You idiot! Your father was never in any scandal! He was as big as ass as you are! I merely concocted that tale to get you out of the way until I should marry. Then, by the terms of our contract, I should be able to control your fortune forever! But now, thanks to a meddlesome strain that seems to run through this *whole* family, I am *nearly* defeated.

HERMAN
But what are you going to do?

BULLFINCH
I am going to kill you. Shoot you down in cold blood.

HERMAN
But the fortune will not go to you, but to Cousin Percy.

BULLFINCH
I'll take care of that fathead when the time comes!

(ENTER CHARLES from behind Bullfinch.)

BULLFINCH (CONT'D)
Now, Herman, prepare to meet your maker!

(CHARLES stabs Bullfinch.)

CHARLES
Die, villain!

(BULLFINCH drops the pistol.)

BULLFINCH
I am done for! Observe me, the victim of my own greed.

(Falls to his knees.)

The web of intrigue that I have spun has now become my winding sheet. Herman! Marry Angeline. Take the Bullfinch fortune that is rightfully yours. But do not ever go to the city! It is an evil place and leads young men to destruction.

(Falls to one elbow.)
BULLFINCH (CONT'D)
Charles, you have been a fool, and I have been so very clever. But what good has it done me? For now I meet a foul, most unnatural, and untimely end. Now I hope to repent all my sins and to gain a place in the after life on the day of judgement.

(CHARLES kneels, facing Bullfinch.)

CHARLES
Oh, oh, oh! Now I see, now that it is too late, now that I too am fading fast, now I see, at your repentance, Archibald, the true beauty of your soul!

BULLFINCH
Oh, oh, oh, Charles! I have been a naughty criminal. But you were wrong as well! Wrong to have been such an irresistible temptation. But I forgive you for your folly, Charles.

*(BULLFINCH tips his hat.
CHARLES tips his hat.)*

CHARLES
And I forgive you your vice, Archibald.

BULLFINCH
Charles!

(He dies.)

                    CHARLES
Archibald!
                    (He dies.)

                    ANGELINE
Herman!

                    HERMAN
Angeline!

                    MR. LOVELY
Wife!

                    MRS. LOVELY
Who, me?

CURTAIN

                    THE END.

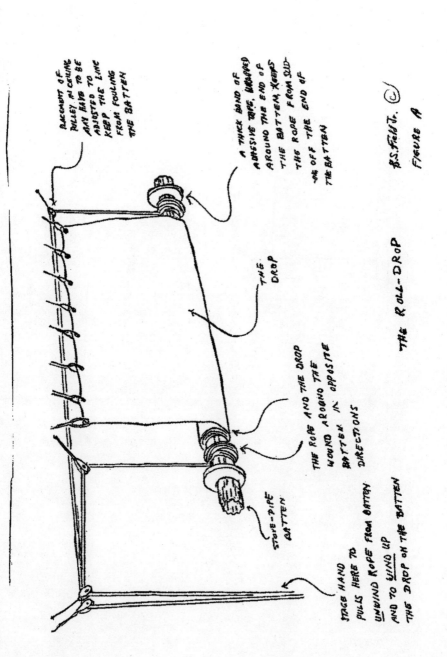

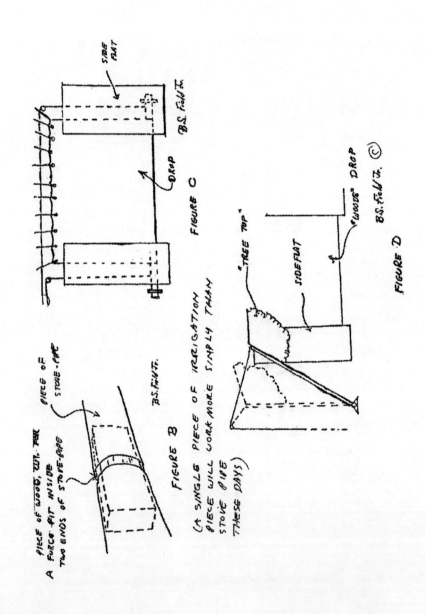

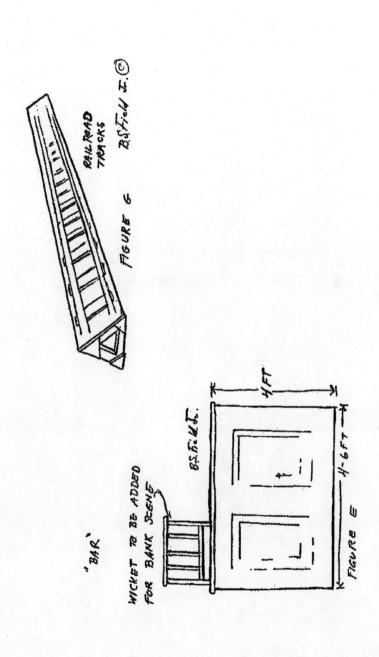

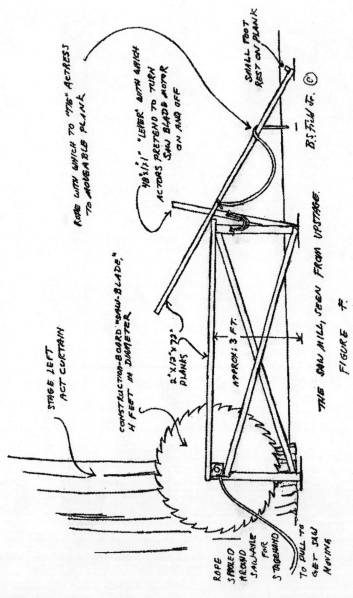

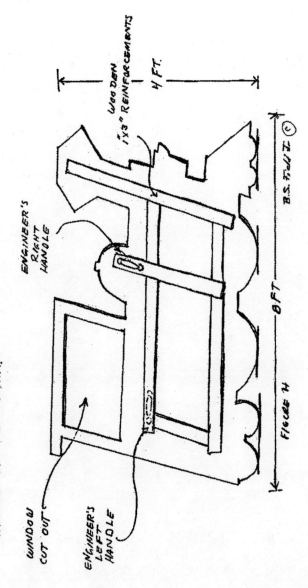

THE HANDLES ARE ONLY APPROXIMATELY PLACED IN THIS PLAN. THE "TRAIN" SHOULD BE FITTED TO THE ACTOR CAST AS THE ENGINEER AS THE ACTOR STANDS WITH HEAD AND LEFT ARM THROUGH THE WINDOW OF THE "TRAIN."

Piece of Work
A philosophic farce in two acts

▼

Persons in the Play

Walter, a government man
Dick, aka Tom, Harry
George, a government man of an opposing government
Jane, daughter of Walter
Sally, George's sister
Camarero, played by the actor of Dick.

Setting:

Time, the present.

Place, two capitol cities on opposite sides of the same river.

THE SCENE: a unit set:
Jane's house, a couch down right in chintz tea roses, or cabbages.
Sally's house, a couch down left, very modern.
Behind each couch, a stand with bottles, glasses, a phone.
Up center, for a café: a table, with three chairs.
Four entrances:
Up right to garage of Jane's house, sometimes an entrance to a government room, sometimes to the café.
Down right, to the rest of Jane's house.
Up left, to front door of Sally's house, sometimes an entrance to the other government's room, sometimes to the café.
Down left, to the rest of Sally's house.

A background of neutral drapes that permits a backstage cross.

Lights to illuminate spaces in use, as needed, and to identify as distinct, the ambience of Jane's house, of Sally's house, of the government rooms, of the café.

Theme music: one tune simply to mark ends of scenes, another to mark longer passages of time, and in the last scene a Latin beat.

No front curtain is needed.

Act I

▼

(AT RISE, Sound: Theme music, anything but NOT a Latin beat, up, then down. Distant typewriters. Enter from right Walter, Dick to table, center.)

WALTER

Sit down.

(Sound: typewriters stop. Walter sits right, Dick left.)

WALTER (Cont'd)

Here, your passport.

(Dick opens passport, reads.)

DICK
What's this? Harry? This isn't me!

WALTER
It is now. Your new name. You'll get used to it.

DICK
Does this mean I'm working for you?

WALTER
Partly. You're a vendor still. Sell stuff to that kraut?

DICK
It's not that simple. Schultz and I are competitors. We both try to sell the same stuff.

(Dick pages through his passport.)

WALTER
Schultz will not be getting a visa.

DICK
I see! I have a visa! Poor Schultz. But without a visa, how can he buy?

WALTER
Schultz can be your retail man. But to avoid the appearance of a cartel, continue to pretend you are competitors. Across the river, you're a buyer, right? From that frog?

DICK

From Dumont.

WALTER

I suppose he'll do. We have a new regime over here now.

DICK

Your Permanent Executive.

WALTER

Glorious Leader is now the preferred title.

DICK

Right! Glorious Leader!

WALTER

He's energetic, like you. Seeks to give his regime an historical meaning. But he has a little trouble with change.

DICK

Know what you mean! I can get you a machine that tells exactly what change to give!

WALTER

Not that kind of change.

DICK

It can be programmed to include various taxes!

WALTER

I don't mean change for money, but just change. He likes permanence.

DICK
Well, sure, I can see now a person might—

WALTER
So, we seem to be clashing with the government across the river.

DICK
That's too bad.

WALTER
It's good for you.

DICK
Oh, I'm glad to hear that.

WALTER
Their tolerance of change across the river—can't tell what they mean. Over here, it makes us nervous

DICK
Don't be nervous. Nervous people shoot guns.

WALTER
We'd like to be calm. So, every time that you come back across the river, let me know. My name is Walter.

DICK
Walter. What do you mean? Let you know? Just to chat? What's the point?

WALTER
Information.

DICK
What do you want to know?

WALTER
I can't tell you that. It's a state secret.

DICK
So, in case they ask me over there, why I'm so nosey, no matter how much they torture me, I won't be tell them what you want.

WALTER
You're very quick. It's symmetrical, isn't it?

DICK
Oh, yeah, aesthetic.

WALTER
I'll know what it means when I hear it, Harry. Later. You may go.

DICK
Right, go! I'm gone.

(Exit both, right.
Sound: Distant typewriters start, then suddenly stop.
Theme music up and then down.
Fade in a babble of distant voices.
Enter George, from left, crosses to table.)

GEORGE
Shut that door behind you.

(Sound: distant babble, typing noise stops.
Enter Dick, right.)

GEORGE (Cont'd)
Sit down.

(Dick sits right.)

GEORGE (Cont'd)
That's nice passport, Sparky.

DICK
They like it at customs.

GEORGE
You go back and forth across the border.

DICK
A shuttle service.

(George puts a passport on the table. Dick picks it up.)

GEORGE
I see you have a visa from them. Now you have one from us.

DICK
And another passport. That'll be handy. My name is Tom?

GEORGE

Objections?

DICK

Uh, I'll get used to it.

GEORGE

What do you sell?

DICK

Electronics. Integrated circuits, zener diodes, small circuit lay-outs—

GEORGE

Never mind the sales pitch! You get all that over here?

DICK

From Dumont.

GEORGE

That Frenchman. Well, none of my business. That's your business. You have to bribe the customs agents?

DICK

Not the ones across the river. Just the ones on this side.

GEORGE

Greedy bastards. Put the bribes down as expenses on your cheat-sheet.

DICK

Cheat-sheet. That means I'm working for you.

GEORGE

Partly. My name is George. Keep your nose clean. For sniffing. That new regime over there is paranoid. We'll debrief you there every time you come back across the border. For starters, we'll use a spare room at Dumont's warehouse. Just ask for me at the counter.

DICK

George? What do you want to know?

GEORGE

Don't get ahead of yourself.

DICK

I don't want to bother bringing back meaningless information.

GEORGE

There's no such thing. That Glorious Leader of theirs has a clamp on any form of information over there.

DICK

So, I just come back and chat.

GEORGE

We'll recognize the meaning of anything you bring.

DICK

The eye of the beholder, hunh?

GEORGE
Until next time, Sparky, er, Tom, was it?

DICK
Tom.

GEORGE
See you.

*(Exit George left.
Sound: Brief surge of distant babble, then stops.)*

DICK
This is getting complicated! And so far it doesn't mean a thing!

*(Dick moves around the table to stage left seat.
Sound: Café music.
Enter Walter right.)*

WALTER
Harry.

DICK
Walter.

WALTER
How's business?

DICK
Not bad.

(Walter sits right.)

WALTER
Not much of a social life.

DICK
No, I keep my nose to—

WALTER
Get a social life over there. Meet people.

DICK
Girls would be nice. Meaningful.

WALTER
Especially if they work for the government.

DICK
Secretaries.

WALTER
We'll keep an eye peeled. We have don't have much information about life over there, but some. I may have some suggestions.

DICK
Sure, I'd like to see some point to it.

WALTER
Meeting in cafés like this is okay for now. We can meet here again next time. But it's a bit open. Their spies over here may read a meaning into it. For ordinary matters, here's a phone number. You can call me any time. From this side of the border. If you have something pressing, come to my office.

DICK

Got it.

WALTER

Call me, time after next.

DICK

Sure.

WALTER

So, after next time, I won't be seeing you, Harry.

DICK

You'll be hearing me. Walter.

WALTER

Right.

(Exit Walter right.
Sound: Café music off.
Dick moves to stage right.
Sound: Distant hammering.
Enter George left.)

GEORGE

How's it going, Tom?

DICK

I'm pretty busy, George.

(Distant hammering stops.)

GEORGE
Must be hard to meet girls over there.

DICK
Actually, I've been too—

GEORGE
With a repressive regime like that one.

DICK
Yeah, maybe that's true.

GEORGE
More open over here. Easier to mix, socially, I mean.

DICK
So far I haven't done much socializing.

GEORGE
There's a girl you should meet.

DICK
Here?

GEORGE
There. Before they changed regimes over there, she and her husband used to like a certain café. She's divorced now, with some kids. I guess it's sort of an intellectual place now. Poetry and stuff like that.

                    DICK
Sounds creepy.

                    GEORGE
It does.

                    DICK
But I'll get used to it.

           (George hands Dick a photo.)

                    GEORGE
Here's a photo. She'd be older now. Her father is in the government. Name on the back.

                    DICK
I get the point.

                    GEORGE
Be nice.

                    DICK
She's kind of good-looking.

                    GEORGE
May be even better now. Enjoy yourself.

                    DICK
I'll try.

GEORGE
One more thing. In my department, it's felt that Dumont's warehouse might be noticed. Their spies might see the point to both of us coming here at once. You have a perfect motive to come here. To buy stuff. But I don't. And I can't stand that constant hammering.

DICK
Dumont's boys are building shipping boxes.

(George offers a piece of paper.)

GEORGE
You can come to my office, if you've got hot news. Here's the address. And that's a phone number. For the usual report, call me. From this side of the border, of course.

DICK
Of course. You will, ah, be hearing from me.

GEORGE
You catch on fast, Sparky, ah, Tom.

*(Exit George, left.
Studies the picture.)*

DICK
This could be tricky. Walter's daughter?

*(Sound: Café music on.
Dick moves to sit left.
Enter Walter right.)*

                    WALTER
Harry.

                    DICK
Hello, Walter.

                    WALTER
Can't linger today.

                    DICK
Next time I'll call you.

            (Walter hands Dick a photo.)

                    WALTER
Here's a name. And a photo. The name's on the back. Meet her.

                    DICK
Where?

                    WALTER
Her brother is in the government.

                    DICK
Uh, over there?

                    WALTER
Of course!

DICK
I get what you mean. Sally...nice looking.

WALTER
Very stylish, they say. A widow. A few kids. Mix over there.

DICK
Socially.

WALTER
Her late husband worked in engineering. She may still move in the same circles. Or maybe not. Look, I've got to go.

DICK
Next time I'll call you, Walter.

(Exit Walter right.)

DICK
I'll be damned! George's sister!

(Enter Jane, right, with a coffee cup.)

DICK
I'll be double-damned! Walter's daughter! Miss? Miss? Are you looking for a seat? I'm just leaving. You can have this table.

JANE
Thank you.

(Jane sits.)

                    DICK
Crowded today.

                    JANE
It is.

                    DICK
You come here often?

                    JANE
No. My Daddy does. Or he used to. He says that, these days, it's effete.

                    DICK
Effete. What's that mean?

                    JANE
The music, I think. Daddy likes marches.

                    DICK
He's in the army.

                    JANE
No. But he's in the government.

                    DICK
I'm a traveling salesman. The name is, ah, Harry.

                    JANE
Pleased to meet you, Harry. My name is Jane.

DICK
I'm pleased to meet you, Jane. But, alas, I have to go. Maybe some other time.

JANE
Yes, Harry. Some other time. I usually come here about this time of day. But it's getting so popular!

DICK
Interesting. Perhaps I'll see you again, Jane.

(Exit Dick left.)

JANE
Damn! Just meet a nice-looking guy, and he has to leave!

(Jane rises.)

JANE (Cont'd)
I don't want this stupid coffee! Well, maybe next time.

*(Exit Jane right.
Sound: Party noise, music.
Enter Sally left, with a glass.
Enter Dick left with a glass.)*

DICK
What's wrong?

SALLY
The style! An aesthetic obscenity!

                    DICK
Aesthetic, hunh? That bothers you a lot?

                    SALLY
Of course! Doesn't it bother you?

                    DICK
It's a little garish.

                    SALLY
Garish! It's a crime against taste.

                    DICK
Well, an open society, Sally, all sorts of stuff gets a work-out.

                    SALLY
Do I know you?

                    DICK
I'm Tom.

                    SALLY
You know my name.

                    DICK
Now you know mine.

                    SALLY
How'd you know my name?

                              DICK
I asked! I saw you, and I said, who's the beauty? And three
guys at once said "Sally!"

                              SALLY
Oh.

                              DICK
So I followed you out here.

                              SALLY
What three guys?

                              DICK
I didn't ask.

                              SALLY
You work for the government?

                              DICK
I'm a traveling salesman.

                              SALLY
Traveling! You mean that you cross the border?

                              DICK
Regularly! A shuttle.

                              SALLY
Is it true that they have intellectual cafés over there?

DICK
They do. Their writers don't dare publish anything with meaning. That government is paranoid about satire. So the writers read it to each other in cafés.

SALLY
I can't get visa to go over there!

DICK
Can't you work a scam?

SALLY
Won't work. My damned brother is in the government here.

DICK
Get him to quit.

SALLY
He keeps getting promoted! Damned nuisance!

DICK
Still, I bet the money's good.

SALLY
I need a refill.

DICK
To cool your temper.

SALLY

Or to fuel it.

*(Exit Sally right.
Sound: party sound and music stops.
Dick crosses table, center, sits stage left.
Sound: Distant typewriters.
Enter Walter stage right.)*

WALTER

You couldn't phone?

(Sound: Distant typewriters stop.)

DICK

I thought you'd want to see my face. More meaningful. I met her.

WALTER

Met Sally?

DICK

Right. A party for some electronic engineers. Her date was one of them.

WALTER

So you horned in?

DICK

Wasn't that what you meant? She thought the style of something clashed.

                    WALTER
What does that mean?

                    DICK
Bad colors? Hell, I don't know. I agreed with her. So we got along well.

                    WALTER
What's she know about their foreign office?

                    DICK
Walter, I never even mentioned her brother.

                    WALTER
But that's the point, to find out what their foreign office is up to.

                    DICK
Well, she mentioned him.

                    WALTER
What'd she say?

                    DICK
She can't get a visa because he's in the government.

                    WALTER
Is that all?

                    DICK
Give me a chance to work on it! It's not her, but her brother that knows stuff. It'll take time!

WALTER
You may be right.

DICK
Take it slow.

WALTER
We're inserting a sleeper.

DICK
A sleeper? I just met her, Walter.

WALTER
I mean you should conduct a normal life over there. Insinuate yourself into the family, and then, later, when we need you, we will call upon. Awake the sleeper.

DICK
Sleeper! I see the meaning!

WALTER
It's a metaphor.

DICK
Sure. I'll call when I have anything meaningful to report.
WALTER
I'll be looking forward to it.

(Exit Walter up right. Sound: Theme music up and then down. Distant typing. Dick moves to stage right chair. Sound: Distant typing stops. Distant voices fade it. Enter George up left. Sound: Distant voices stop.)

GEORGE
This better be good, Sparky.

DICK
Something meaningful, George.

GEORGE
At least there's no hammering here in our offices.

DICK
Your tip on the intellectual café was on the money.

GEORGE
You met Jane?

DICK
Yeah, I met her.

GEORGE
When do you see her again?

DICK
Come on, George, I don't have a date. Not yet.

GEORGE
Get to work on it, Tom!

DICK
I will, don't worry.

GEORGE
What did you talk about?

DICK
We didn't talk about anything!

GEORGE
What was the point?

DICK
I told her my name, she told me hers. And she told me right off that her father's in the government.

GEORGE
What did you say about yourself?

DICK
No problem, I told her I was a traveling salesman.

GEORGE
Oh, swell, that's a heavy come-on!

DICK
Hey, it's the truth! Nothing wrong with the truth!

GEORGE
As long as it doesn't get in the way.

DICK
She knows I'm making money. Their Glorious Leader told the Americans to take a hike, and now his regime can't get electronic parts.

GEORGE

That's true.

DICK

Except from me and from Schultz. Look, I didn't come talk business, just to tell you I met this Jane. I'll see her again some time.

GEORGE

When?

DICK

Some time! I don't know. You get too eager, you'll spoil it.

GEORGE

I see your meaning. Take it slow.

DICK

I could be a sleeper, hunh?

GEORGE

When we need to know something meaningful later on...

DICK

Right, later on, right.

GEORGE

Then we can wake you up. Fine! Gotta split. Keep me in touch. Use the phone!

                    DICK
Look there's a complication—

*(Exit George up left. Sound: Distant babble of voices,
starts, stops. Café music begins.
Enter Jane up right, comes to put a hand on his shoulder.)*

                    JANE
Hi, Harry.

                    DICK
Hi, Jane.

            (Jane bends to kiss him, then sits left.)

                    JANE
How do you feel?

                    DICK
Me? Great!

                    JANE
I mean, after last night.

                    DICK
That's what I mean, great after last night.

                    JANE
Harry, are you married?

                    DICK
No, Jane, I'm not. What makes you ask?

JANE
I've heard that salesman traveling salesmen have a girl in every market.

DICK
I know some girls in other markets. I'll admit it. But I never married any of them.

JANE
A girl wonders.

DICK
Only one reason a girl would wonder that.

JANE
Don't be cute, Harry.

DICK
Being cute suits my personality. Yours too, I think. Are you married?

JANE
I told you about that. He left.

DICK
He left you with those neat girls.

JANE
I'd never have let him take them along.

                    DICK
You want to propose to me?

                    JANE
That is cute.

                    DICK
I thought so.

                    JANE
You waiting for me to ask?

                    DICK
Guess.

                    JANE
Harry, will you marry me?

                    DICK
Have you talked it over with your father?

                    JANE
Harry, you're too cute.

                    DICK
Shall I get down on one knee or do you want to?

                    JANE
You're making fun of me.

                    DICK
No, I'm not. I am truly worried that your father will kill me if he finds out that I'm even thinking sexy about you.

JANE

Are you?

DICK

Sure. Isn't it obvious?

JANE

Harry, I asked you a question, seems like hours ago!

DICK

The answer is yes. Kiss me.

(They stand, kiss.)

DICK

Now you have to spring it on your father.

JANE

Daddy will be all right.

DICK

He will foam at the mouth.

JANE

Why? You never met him.

DICK

He's crazy about you, right? Is he gonna let you marry a traveling salesman? It'll never work!

                    JANE

I'll make it work.

                    DICK

Never work.

                    JANE

My girls will start working on their grandpa. Never fear.

                    DICK

I have make some calls. See you again, soon.

                    JANE

Real soon, Harry. I get here after lunch.

                    DICK

Sure thing, after noon, real soon.

> *(They exit right. Harry re-enters, right.*
> *Sound: Café music off.*
> *Dick picks up right phone, dials.)*

               DICK (Cont'd)

Walter? No, we have to meet. Yes, it's meaningful! Got a spanner in the works! Not over there, over here. I can't describe it. It's indescribable. We can use that café again. Morning. Early morning. Won't take long. I'd guess we'll be done real quick!

> *(Sound: Theme music up and down. Dick hangs up,*
> *crosses to left.)*

DICK

It's never gonna work!

(Enter Sally down left.)

DICK (Cont'd)

Hey, Sally!

SALLY

Hello, Tom. When did you get back?

DICK

Yesterday. I called, but your boys told me you had to go. To an opening?

SALLY

Of an art gallery. I'm a patron.

DICK

You give the artist money?

SALLY

Better than give. I buy the artist's work. Trouble is, after my husband died, my boys and I moved in with George. He can stand the boys, barely, but he's insensitive to the aesthetic. He hates art. Doesn't want it around the house.

DICK

You need a house of your own.

SALLY

Is that a proposal?

DICK

Hey, don't be so quick!

SALLY

Never mind. The guys I like always turn out to be the ones who never commit. I only snagged my late husband by getting pregnant. It's defect in my taste.

DICK

I get the feeling that you like me.

SALLY

You get the feeling! You never felt me yet!

DICK

No, not yet. Isn't this sudden?

SALLY

An aesthetic reaction comes from a good piece. Some of these buyers, they walk around, talk about it, is it gonna work? How will it look over the fire place? Maybe on the long wall?

DICK

You think a long engagement is a dumb thing?

SALLY

Tom, if it looks like it's going to work, why not? You never get second chance at a first impression.

(They embrace.)

DICK

I see what you mean!

SALLY

You don't see a thing. All you got, Tom, is glands.

DICK

Glands are good. You got some too!

SALLY

Glad you like 'em. I'm a widow, but I'm also an orphan, Tom. You'll have to talk to my brother, George.

DICK

George. The one in the government.

SALLY

He's not gonna be happy that I picked a traveling salesman, but he'll get used to it.

DICK

What about the boys?

SALLY

The boys dig you already! The sooner we get George started, the sooner he'll quit squealing. He has the taste of a bull-dog.

DICK

You mean he bites?

SALLY

He chews his food forever! As if he thinks that getting it all ragged around the edges will change the flavor.

DICK

A bull-dog.

SALLY

Don't worry. Trust me. You can't trust him, 'cause he changes his ideas according to whatever he heard from the last government big shot who spoke to him.

(She kisses him.)

SALLY (Cont'd)

Gotta run, sweetheart. Give George a call. He's in the directory. I'll prime the boys, and start to work on George on my end. You gnaw on him from the other. It's dull work, but it works.

(Exit Sally left. Dick crosses to table, sits stage left. Enter Walter right. Sound: Café music.)

WALTER

Harry.

DICK

Walter.

WALTER

What's the big mystery?

                    DICK

I've had some proposals.

                    WALTER

From them?

                    DICK

From women.

                    WALTER

Really?

                    DICK

Sort of shocked me, really.

                    WALTER

That Sally?

                    DICK

Yes.

                    WALTER

Wonderful! When's the wedding?

                    DICK

We're working on it. Her brother is a problem. You know, having his sister married to a traveling salesman?

                    WALTER

If he only knew!

                    DICK
Let's hope he never does.

                    WALTER
Well, of course.

                    DICK
And one other.

                    WALTER
Other what?

                    DICK
Other woman.

                    WALTER
My god, Harry, you got two over there?

                    DICK
One over here.

                    WALTER
Over here? What in hell did you do that for?

                    DICK
I didn't do it! She proposed to me! I was flattened!

                    WALTER
Well, get rid of her!

                    DICK
Not that easy. She's real set on it. Talk to her.

WALTER

Me? Do I know her?

DICK

Yes. I met her right here.

WALTER

Here?

DICK

Jane.

WALTER

My daughter?

DICK

Talk to her, Walter!

WALTER

You've been trying to seduce my Jane?

DICK

Talk her out of marrying me, Walter.

WALTER

I sure as hell will!

DICK

Great!

WALTER

You don't want my daughter?

DICK

I love her, Walter. That's the point! I don't want to marry her if I'm committed over there! I'm supposed to be a pipeline from Sally's brother to your ear.

WALTER

Damn! I've been promoting your connection to Sally with Our Glorious Leader! Can't pull the plug on it now!

DICK

Right. Settle it. Keep your daughter away from me.

WALTER

Jane is going to get a piece of my mind!

DICK

Great.

(Exit Walter, right.)

DICK

I hope it works. That Jane, she seems quiet, and nice, and easy-going. But she may have an arm-hold on her father. Lots of women do.

(Exit Dick up left. Sound: Café music off. Enter Walter and Jane down right. Use the right couch as their acting area.)

JANE
Let me make you a drink, Daddy.

(Jane goes behind the couch to glasses and bottles.)

WALTER
After all, Jane, a traveling salesman!

JANE
Is that the policy of the new regime, to insist on class distinctions?

WALTER
No! Dammit, this isn't about politics.

JANE
No, it's about husbands.

WALTER
But this man—

JANE
You've met him?

WALTER
I can't be sure.

JANE
You were sure about my ex-husband. You were all in favor of that marriage. And you were wrong.

WALTER

Dammit, girl—

JANE

Here's your drink.

WALTER

Don't take me up short every time—

JANE

Harry is a nice man. My girls think, and I quote, "that he's cool, he's boss!" Let's go out and sit in the garden. If I like him, the girls like him, how meaningful is an opinion with a track record like yours, Daddy?

WALTER

I resent the implications...

(Jane, Walter exit down right, as they finish their lines off stage. Sound: Theme music up, then down. George, Sally enter up left.)

GEORGE

No, I forbid it!

SALLY

Forbid and be damned!

GEORGE

You can't marry this guy!

SALLY
What's got into you?

GEORGE
I got the ministry.

SALLY
Oh. So now you're top dog at Foreign Affairs.

GEORGE
And my sister getting married to a traveling salesman—

SALLY
Wouldn't look good?

GEORGE
It wouldn't.

SALLY
What a crock! You got the ministry now, George. You don't have to worry the meaning of everything you do any more!

GEORGE
I have to worry about it even more!

SALLY
Try and stop me, George!

GEORGE
Sally, this is a delicate political question.

SALLY
An oxymoron. All political questions are indelicate!

GEORGE
You don't understand the ramifications!

SALLY
I damn well understand that I'm getting no ramifications now!

GEORGE
This guy, this traveling salesman—

SALLY
Is capable of very effective ramifications.

GEORGE
Don't talk like that!

SALLY
I'm a widow, George. I have a shooting-license! Ever since my husband smashed himself to bits on that damned motorcycle, I have been sleeping alone. And now the boys are heading off for college. Come on out in the kitchen. I need a drink.

GEORGE
You are making the situation very difficult...

(Exit George, Sally down left. finish their last lines off stage. Sound: Theme music up, then down. Enter Dick up left, goes to phone, dials, maybe sits on the left couch.)

DICK
George? Hi, I have some news. What? Oh, thanks, but the boys are the ones who should get the congratulations, for graduating.

(Phone on stage right rings.)

DICK (Cont'd)
Look, some news. I'm just back from across the border.

(Phone on stage right rings.)

DICK (Cont'd)
Their Glorious Leader over there passed a Wassermann test.

(Phone on stage right rings.)

DICK (Cont'd)
Right! It means he had to take one, George!

(Enter Jane, down right, goes to phone and answers it.)

JANE
Hello?

DICK
Well, it's not big news—but remember, George, you heard it from me first.

JANE

No, no, Daddy, he's not back yet.

DICK

I'll bet you don't hear it from them at all!

(Dick hangs up the phone, exits up left.)

JANE

Yes, isn't it exciting? Both girls got proposals! Of course it didn't hurt that they both had dowries. Dowries, Daddy! No, of course you didn't. You never thought of it. But Harry did, from the day we set the date on our marriage, he began to provide for theirs. Harry thinks ahead, Daddy.

(Enter Dick up right, comes to Jane.)

JANE

He's here now, Daddy. (to Dick) It's Daddy. He was calling to talk to you.

(They kiss briefly, and Dick takes the phone. Jane sits on the couch.)

DICK

Hello, Walter? Harry here. Well, not much. A promotion. In their Foreign Affairs ministry. A guy named George—yeah, that's the one. He's to be the new minister. What? Oh, dowries? I'm doing pretty well, Walter. I got nearly a monopoly on the traffic in small electronic parts across the border. Thanks to, ah, conditions. What? Oh, sure. Keep it quiet. Sure thing. Well, congratulations on the

DICK
good thing. And condolences on the bad ones. Yeah, you'll be hearing from me.

(Dick puts an arm around Jane.)

JANE
What was that about?

DICK
This is a hug.

(Pulls her to him.)

JANE
You can't tell about it? Daddy made you promise?

DICK
Don't tell your girls. Grandpa is the new Interior Minister!

JANE
He'll be so proud! What happened to the old one?

DICK
Cabinet re-shuffle. Because our Glorious Leader...he's sick, Jane. Bad. Sexual stuff.

JANE
That sounds terrible! What will it mean if he dies?

DICK
Good question. No one knows. No one has the guts to prepare for it. Suppose he recovers! That's the point! Uncertainty is bad for business. No one knows that he's sick, yet.

(Dick rises.)

DICK (Cont'd)
I need to sell some stuff. Buy some. When the news is out, prices of stocks will fall like rocks. Prices of equipment will go up like balloons.

*(Exit Dick up right.
Jane rises.)*

JANE
I better warn those girls to spend their dowries wisely!

(Exit Jane down right. Sound: Theme music up, then down. Enter George. Dick up left.)

DICK
My god, are all the meetings like that?

GEORGE
Like what?

DICK
That stuff about Felton.

GEORGE
Felton's a hard man, but efficient.

DICK
Termination! That is hard!

GEORGE
Government is the business of making hard decisions.

DICK
I hope I never get tangled up with that.

GEORGE
Sorry if that stuff offends you. What have you got for us?

DICK
Jane's father is to be the new Minister of the Interior over there.

GEORGE
Great! We'll have an inside line on everything! Getting you married to that woman is the smartest work I've done!

DICK
Glad you're glad, because there's more.

GEORGE
How badly did the former minister screw up? Wasn't he a cousin of their so-called Glorious Leader?

DICK
A nephew. He's been promoted to Minister for Foreign affairs.

GEORGE
That jerk in the foreign office?

DICK
There's to be a general cabinet shuffle. The minister of health is out. Fled the country.

GEORGE
What did he do?

DICK
He was in charge of the State Pathology Lab. Remember the Wassermann test of the Glorious Leader?

GEORGE
He passed it.

DICK
Nope. He flunked it. Except that the State Pathologist was too incompetent to read the results right. So, the Glorious Leader may not live long.

GEORGE
This will mean big changes!

DICK
Hard to guess what's next.

(Exit George, Dick up left. Sound: Theme music up, then down. Enter Dick down right.)

DICK
Jane, I've got to go.

(Enter Jane down right.)

JANE
You always eat and run!

DICK
At least I stayed to eat the meal!

JANE
You peek at my menu and then decide whether to stay or not!

DICK
I stayed in spite of the threat from Schultz, who will steal my customers if I don't get to work!

JANE
Schultz! It's hard to believe. Frau Schultz is such a nice woman.

DICK
Glad you like her. Meanwhile, her husband wants to gobble me alive.

JANE
Harry, we need to make plans!

DICK
For what?

JANE
To finish re-decorating this house, now that the girls have moved out.

DICK
How much more is this going to cost?

JANE
You can't just leave the rooms in the mess the girls left.

DICK
What mess?

JANE
Have you even looked, Harry? Did you ever look?

DICK
Jane, the money, not the girls, is the issue here!

JANE
Well, they weren't boys, so you never had a moment for them!

DICK
I never left you! I stayed! I was trying to make money!

JANE
Money, that's all you think about!

DICK
I made money. Their husbands were happy to see the girls coming down the aisle!

JANE
Now don't start on those two boys!

DICK
They got the girls, they got the dowries! It's supposed to cost us less to live now, not more!

JANE
But the rooms are so awful!

DICK
They're fine!

JANE
You're so insensitive!

DICK
And I'm gone.
(Dick exits up right.)

JANE
Harry! Dammit, come back here! That damned man! I wanted to show him some samples! Why does he always rush off like that? What does that mean?

*(Jane exits down right.
Enter Dick up left, in a black derby.)*

DICK
Sally, Sally, I'm home!

(Enter Sally down left.)

DICK
Sorry I'm late, but I had meeting across the river, held me up.

SALLY
I hope you're not expecting a meal at this hour.

DICK
No, just a little—

SALLY
I ate by myself—

DICK
—show of warmth when I do get home.

SALLY
—a little salad, some tea, while knowing that you are across the border, with those cosmopolitan aesthetes you know—

DICK
Come on, aesthetes!

SALLY
Everyone knows life is more elegant over there!

DICK
Aesthetes! They're engineers!

SALLY

Where did you get that dreadful hat?

DICK

Oh, the derby?

SALLY

Makes you looking working-class.

DICK

I know it's not aesthetic, but it's for my work! A kind of an i.d. when I cross the border.

SALLY

Doesn't George get you a visa for that?

DICK

There are two sets of border guards at the bridge! Ours and theirs. The visa keeps the other side's guards happy, but ours are always looking for a bribe.

SALLY

Tell my brother about it!

DICK

George can stop it for one trip, but they start holding me up for pay-off again the next day. Anyway, the derby does means I'm cool.

SALLY

That damned hat is not cool!

DICK
To our border guards, it means I've already paid, and it's cool.

SALLY
It's gauche!

DICK
It's the meaning that counts, not the style!

SALLY
Style is the essence of meaning!

DICK
Sally! I need to get back and forth across the border quick. The stuff that Dumont sells me is red-hot and new for only so long.

SALLY
I will be humiliated if Madame Dumont sees you in that stupid hat!

DICK
I have competitors who are trying to beat me to the market!

SALLY
When you retire, get me a visa too!

DICK
Uh, that may not work.

SALLY

George was saying he's heard talk that might mean peace treaty.

DICK

Pooh, doesn't mean a thing! Talk, talk...

SALLY

It'd mean we could sell this dump, and travel!

DICK

Hey, it's not a dump.

SALLY

Paris, London, New York!

DICK

You raised three boys here!

SALLY

And all three are out of the nest!

DICK

Peter is still in college!

SALLY

He's moved out of this house, Tom. Fred's in graduate school, and Robert is working, married, has his own life. You'll be a step-grandfather one day!

DICK

But selling the house!

SALLY

Location! We live in a relentlessly provincial city—I don't care if it's the capitol of a country—it's a hick town!

DICK

But it's a wonderful—

SALLY

Place to bring up kids! They're all brought up! We're rattling around in this old barn like peas in a whistle.

DICK

You've decorated it with such style!

SALLY

My god, that's the first time I've heard that you noticed! And who else in this dopey burg could appreciate it? Madame Dumont! That drip?

DICK

You always got along with her—

SALLY

Come on, Tom! Madame Dumont is the wife of your most important vendor! Of course I get along with her. You want something to eat, you'll have to come out to the kitchen and forage for yourself.

(Exit Sally down left, continues off.)

SALLY (CONT'D, OFF)
You don't see the meaning of anything! Nothing! How you ever managed to survive selling electronic gadgets, let alone prosper, has been a continual mystery to me!

*(Exit Dick down left.
Sound: Theme music up, then out. Stage right phone rings.
Enter Jane from down right, answers phone.)*

JANE
Daddy! How are you? Things at the ministry going along? Harry? He's due back any minute. You know, Harry might retire soon. That means, now that the nest is empty, we could re-do the place.

(Enter Dick, up right, holding newspaper.)

JANE
And the garden too. It needs a lot of work just to maintain, Daddy.

DICK
Let me talk to him.

JANE
Daddy? It's Harry. He just came in. You want to—well, yes. Harry? It's Daddy. At the ministry. Something's up, I suppose.

DICK
Hello, sir. Right, I've got it in my hands. Well, of course I never believe anything in print, but—(Pause) You mean it's true? (Pause) Liable to be true?

JANE
What's in the paper that's true?

DICK
Yes, that means big changes! I can guess. Me? No, I'm not worried! Why would I be worried? Right. I'll check in later.

(Hangs up)

JANE
Dammit, Harry, I was just talking to Daddy and you hung up the phone!

DICK
Look at that headline. First page, bottom.

JANE
A peace treaty?

DICK
Right.

JANE
It would be a relief, after all these years. I can never remember what the two countries are supposed to have against each other.

DICK
They've been teaching it in school.

JANE

Well, you know how much attention anyone pays to the stuff they teach in school!

DICK

This may mean big changes in business.

JANE

You may not even need a visa to cross the border.

DICK

Might mean that no one will need a visa. When it was impossible to get one, your father arranged one for me. But if no one needs one, that means that everyone can cross the border at will!

JANE

Oh, you mean your competitors—

DICK

Schultz will put me out of business!

JANE

Why don't you retire, Harry? We could work on this house. On the garden, too!

DICK

See you later.

(Exit Dick up right.)

JANE

Lazy-bones! The minute I mention work in the garden, you find some excuse to beat it. All because of some nonsense in this stupid paper!

*(Exit Jane with paper down right.
Sound: Theme music up, then fades.
Enter Sally down left.)*

SALLY

It means that she'll have to have him cremated. What a time for him to get killed. Just as we have a peace treaty. We'll be able to cross the border to shop.

GEORGE

As I've said, it seems that he was a spy. For the other side.

SALLY

Well, the poor man is dead. Beyond caring.

GEORGE

So they will refuse his widow the pension.

SALLY

Oh, no, the poor thing. How can they be so cruel?

GEORGE

Well, they can't be seen to countenance treachery.

SALLY

Don't recite your political rubbish to me, George! It's all bullshit and you know it.

(Enter Dick up left, with derby, breathless.)

SALLY

Tom!

DICK

Hello, George. Don't often see you here.

GEORGE

Hello, Tom. Look, Sally, I gotta go.

SALLY

Coward!

GEORGE

Tom, see you later some time.

SALLY

Leaving me to do the explaining!

(Exit George up right.)

DICK

Explaining what?

SALLY

Madame Dumont will be swindled out of her pension.

DICK

Madame Dumont?

SALLY
Dumont died, turned out to be a spy, double agent, traitor, some rubbish that George was repeating like a damned parrot. All an excuse to avoid paying the widow.

DICK
Dumont's dead?

SALLY
Someone found the body. By the river. But you haven't heard the good news. They are signing a peace treaty! Tomorrow. Us and those across the river!

DICK
How'd he die?

SALLY
Isn't it great? That means that we can shop over there at last.

DICK
What about Dumont?

SALLY
Rub shoulders with all those intellectuals in their coffee shops!

DICK
Dumont! What happened to him?

SALLY
Something grotesque. Head and hands cut off. Seems hard, but if she has him cremated, no one will know.

DICK

Head and hands!

SALLY

This mean that real estate prices over here will sky-rocket! The perfect time to sell this barn!

DICK

Jesus! Felton! I gotta go!

SALLY

Tom, you just got here!

*(Exit Dick up left.
Enter Jane down right, holding a phone.)*

JANE

No, Daddy, he's not here but—

SALLY

Men! They get so overexcited at the slightest news.

JANE

But the last time you called, we got cut off!

SALLY

The boys are like that, a football score, and they're off!

JANE

I was explaining my plans, Daddy!

SALLY
Men! I wonder if Tom has been betting on something?

(Exit Sally down left.)

JANE
For redecoration, of course! (Pause) I'll tell Harry when he comes in!

(Enter Dick up right, breathing heavily.)

JANE (Cont'd)
Here he is now, Daddy! Harry? It's Daddy. He wants to talk to you.

DICK
God, now what? (Takes the phone) Hello, sir?

JANE
Every time Daddy calls me, he just wants to talk to you!

DICK
Yes, sir, we were—Oh.

JANE
I just wanted to talk about my re-decoration plans.

DICK
Uh, yeah. What?

JANE
Redecoration.

					DICK
The head? The hands? Then how does anyone know—oh.

					JANE
And the garden, too!

					DICK
Felton. Right, confirmation.

					JANE
Getting new plants.

					DICK
Right.

					JANE
Some better manure.

					DICK
Right. (Hangs up.)

					JANE
What was so important?

					DICK
Schultz is dead.

					JANE
Schultz? Your competitor?

DICK
They found the body by the river.

JANE
Did you kill him, Harry?

DICK
No head, no hands, just the body. They identified him by his clothes, his papers. Felton.

JANE
Without a head?

DICK
Felton.

JANE
I thought you said Mister Schultz. Who's Felton?

DICK
An assassin. Works by contract. Felton always cuts off the head and hands, sends them to his employer to prove that he got the right man. So that's how they found Schultz.

JANE
Oh, poor Frau Schultz!

DICK
You know her?

JANE
We both do garden club. The poor woman! We have to go over to her place right now!

DICK
I've got to go. I may be late for supper.

(Exit Dick up right.)

JANE
Harry! Harry! You coward! Running out when it gets awkward!

(Sound: theme music up then down. Dick, moving with desperation, enters up left. He wears a derby.)

DICK
Sally? Sally, are you home?

(Dick exits down left.)

DICK (Off)
Sally?

(Dick enters down left.)

DICK
Just when I need her! Out shopping or something.

(Dick grabs the stage left phone, punches buttons.)

DICK
George! Maybe her brother knows what it means. Come on, come on, pick up the damned—George! It's me, ah, Tom! George, I just saw Felton! Yes, Felton. (Pause) Don't

DICK

gimme that line of bullshit! Felton did a job for your boys. (Pause) Schultz, that's who! (Pause) How do I know? Dammit, George, I was in the meeting when they decided—yes, now you got it!

(Jane enters up right, dressed for an afternoon of shopping, carrying a cup and saucer, crosses to the table, center, and sits.)

DICK (Cont'd)

Oh, well, just called to chat about it, George, just pleasant gossip about the meaning of it all. I think that fucker Felton has me on his list. Yes, me! What about Dumont? Same m.o.! Felton did him too! For the other side, that's who! Yeah? Yeah, do that, check—check into it? Sure thing. See you.

(Dick hangs up.)

DICK (Cont'd)

George, that bastard! Shit, I gotta—gotta do what? If that Felton gets close, he'll—he may know I'm here. George will check on it, will he? I can guess what that means! George is on the phone with Felton now, telling him where to find me! I wonder if Walter knows anything?

(Dick picks up the phone, hits numbers.)

DICK ()

No, dammit!

(Dick slams the phone back down again.)

DICK ()
Not from this side of the border! Gotta get back across the bridge. Gotta keep moving!

(Exit Dick up left.
Sound: Theme music up, then out. Enter Sally up right,
dressed in more elegant style than
Jane, with cup and saucer.)

SALLY
Excuse me, Madame? May I share your table?

JANE
Of course! Sit down.

SALLY
So crowded in here, isn't it?

JANE
It always is.

SALLY
You come here often?

JANE
Yes, I do. Three, four times a week. I meet—I used to meet friends here.

SALLY
Are you an intellectual?

JANE

Hardly!

SALLY

One hears that this is a highly intellectual coffee shop.

JANE

I come for the coffee.

SALLY

That seems to be good, too.

JANE

This is your first time here?

SALLY

First time this side of the river.

JANE

The border!

SALLY

Yes, the border. Now that international tensions have been relaxed, I thought I'd, well...

JANE

Look around.

SALLY

Rather like a tourist. Almost like an American!

JANE
Isn't it a relief! That all that international nonsense is over?

SALLY
My husband's relieved. And my brother.

JANE
My husband too. My father's in the government over here. Ministry of the Interior. He keeps trying to explain to me why we ever did get into such a snit with your country, but...

SALLY
I get the same stuff from my brother. George is in our foreign ministry.

JANE
So we're both from the diplomatic world! My name is Jane!

(Enter Dick up right, exhausted, terrified. He wears no hat. He has a package of ice cream in his hands, hurries around the end of Jane's couch, turning back to down right.)

SALLY
My pleasure, Jane. My name is Sally.

DICK
Jane? Jane are you home? It's me, Harry!

SALLY
It's a pleasure to meet you, Jane.

DICK
Hm! Out shopping. What can I move to make things fit?

JANE
It's only fitting that we women meet to discuss foreign affairs, not just for shopping, planning menus.

DICK
Wonder what's on her menu for tonight.

(Exit Dick down right with ice cream.)

SALLY
It's wonder that men can make any sense about politics. My brother, George, used to give me his propaganda about the suspicions between nations. It doesn't mean a thing!

JANE
Men!

SALLY
Men!

(Enter Dick down right, empty-handed, to rush around Jane's couch toward up right exit.)

DICK
What a meal she's planning! That means she'll need meat!

(Exit Dick up right.)

SALLY
I will say, my husband sees no need for such double-talk. it all.

JANE
My Harry doesn't either.

SALLY
No need to believe any of that stuff, Tom says. But even if it's meaningless, it has it's effects. He has learned to repeat the phrases, memorizes them until he has them cold.

(Enter Dick up right, with a two lumps wrapped in white butcher paper.)

DICK
These are cold! I can get one in the kitchen freezer, let the other thaw.

(Exit Dick down right.)

SALLY
A political thaw, Tom says, would make things hard. Now, of course, he has a visa to cross the border. He sells electronic things, and has good customers over here.

JANE
Harry sells electronics too! Perhaps our husbands know each other!

SALLY
Wouldn't surprise me!

(Enter Dick down right.)

DICK
One more load should do it!

(Exit Dick up right.)

JANE
One more coincidence! Though, Harry is about to retire.

SALLY
So is Tom! I can hardly wait, too see Paris, London, New York.

JANE
Oh, Harry and I will not budge!

(Enter Dick up right with more white bundles.)

DICK
Some of it's too big to budge, but I can leave it where it is for now. Glad I bought an oversize freezer for the garage! Who would ever have thought...

(Exit Dick down right.)

JANE
I've thought a lot about getting that house finished, at last.

(Enter Dick down right.)

DICK
And now with any luck there's room for the body!

(Exit Dick up right.)

JANE
Lots of room there now. The girls are married and out of it. That means that I can get rid of the clutter, fix up a sewing room, and work in my garden!

(Enter Dick up right. He grabs phone from behind the couch, dials, eventually sits on the couch.)

SALLY
My boys are out of the nest too. One's married, works at a job, one's in grad school. We hardly see them, just talk by phone.

DICK
This is Harry. Right.

SALLY
The last one's just starting college now, but, really that means that he's gone too. Tom and I rattle around in that big dump like peas in a whistle.

DICK
Is Walter available? Give him a whistle, can you? Thanks.

SALLY

Now that peace has broken out, so to speak, real estate prices on our side of the border are starting to rise! As soon as Tom retires, we're going to sell and hit the road. Every morning we'll see new sights.

DICK

Ah, good morning, sir! Harry here. Right.

SALLY

I'd love to play golf in America, tennis too, and do some scuba diving.

JANE

Oh, Sally, you're much more sporting that I am!

DICK

It's more that that! Something's gone wrong. You remember that hired assassin, Felton?

JANE

Now that you're here, do you have anything special planned?

DICK

That's right. You planned for him to do Schultz for us. And they had him do Dumont for them.

JANE

Art galleries? Museums? Certain paintings to see you can identify?

DICK
Did anyone identify either of those bodies beyond the papers on them?

SALLY
I hoped to meet some intellectuals, I suppose. That's why I came to this coffee shop.

DICK
I know, budget cuts mean that the smart scientists have left for better jobs. The police forensic labs are pretty primitive. Our Glorious Leader died because the State Pathologist was too incompetent to read a Wassermann test. Not likely that he can manage a meaningful test for DNA!

JANE
What you mean, intellectuals? What do they look like?

DICK
Well, with no hands, and no head, not much more than the papers to go on.

SALLY
Look like? I don't know. Beards, berets, I guess.

DICK
Sure, the head, the hands and the hands prove he's got the right victim.

JANE
Oh, yes, beards, berets. Actually, I don't think they come out until dark.

                    DICK
How does he send them—

                    SALLY
Maybe I could come back here later, after dinner.

                    DICK
Styrofoam package!

                    SALLY
Though, since there's only Tom at home now, dinner is nothing more than a few drinks, and then tuna-fish salad and soup.

                    DICK
Any fishmonger can supply it! And with dry ice! Felton patron's pays off as soon as he gets the package.

                    JANE
I'll bet that pays off in keeping your figure. I've been cooking great chunks of meat since the girls got married. Salad and soup, that's so sensible!

                    DICK
It makes sense here. Felton has been hanging around. Not just over there, but over here, too.

                    JANE
Never could, while the girls were still at home. Worried about their figures, you know.

DICK
The decrease in international tension has made me feel, well, like surplus goods. You could just fire me, of course, but, considering what I know, I thought you might maybe just have decided on termination?

SALLY
That big dump of mine is empty now.

DICK
You decided not to, or you haven't decided?

JANE
I'm sure it's not a dump! Just to look at you, the way you dress, I know the house is considered in the highest taste!

DICK
You wouldn't consider it! Well, thank you, sir!

SALLY
Thank you, but maybe you should see for yourself. It's not that hard to cross the border these days.

DICK
A vote of confidence! That is a wonderful relief!

JANE
Why Sally, that would be wonderful. But since you're already on this side, why not have a look at my house. And the garden!

DICK

Yes sir! Thank you, sir!

(Dick jumps up, puts down the phone.)

DICK

The bastard!

SALLY

Jane, I'm in your city for the first time in my life, and—

DICK

Vote of confidence!

JANE

But of course you'll come by my place!

DICK

Just what they probably told Schultz and Dumont.

SALLY

Don't you think we would check with the people in Protocol first?

DICK

Just before they had Felton kill them. The old devil is putting my ass on the line!

JANE

And would we ever get permission? Would we ever get an answer?

DICK

My head on the block! Wouldn't consider a termination! Ha! The old liar! Hands, finger-prints. And the head! If I got rid of those....

(Dick exits up right.)

SALLY

No answer means "no."

JANE

But if we don't ask, they can't even say "no" by not answering!

(Sound: off-stage right, a band-saw grinding.)

SALLY

Well, if you insist...

JANE

I do! My garden's not finished yet, of course, but then a garden never is!

SALLY

You're so kind, Jane!

(Sally looks around. Jane looks around. Sound: Band saw stops.)

JANE

No sign of a waiter.

SALLY
They're very slow at presenting the bill here.

JANE
Let's just go to the counter and pay on our way out.

(Jane and Sally exit up right. Sound: Theme music up and down. Enter Dick up left, with derby on, holding two packages..)

DICK
Sally? Sally? Here I am! Gone again? Or still.

(Enter Sally, Jane up right.)

JANE
And here we are! I hope you can see why we like it so!

DICK
Disposall. Sally has a disposall in the kitchen.

(Exit Dick down left.)

SALLY
Yes, I think I can....

(Sally looks over the cabbage/rose chintz decor. She disapproves.)

JANE
It's really homey the way Harry and I like it.

SALLY

I see what you mean by "homey."

(Sound: From off left, the screech of a disposall under stress, off and on.)

JANE

Do you garden? No, you said you didn't have the space. Or the time. We garden. Come look at the garden. It's so pretty. All the flowers. We like just to look at it.

SALLY

One must, I suppose.

JANE

We are out there every day. Well, not when it rains. But even when it rains, we can stand inside and look at it. We stand right here. See, out there. When it rains, each of the flowers nods its head at us, whenever a drop hits it, you see.

SALLY

Jane, I have rather a different kind of decor as an ideal at my house. You must come and see it! I find that I am quite devoted to the primacy of style.

JANE

The primacy of it? Of style?

SALLY

Come see it now! Today.

JANE

I really ought to get started making dinner.

SALLY

Come, now, Jane. Let's have no feeble excuses. It's hardly mid-afternoon.

(Sally moves up right.)

JANE

Really, I'd love to come over! Harry will have to snack until I get back here to make the meal.

SALLY

My Tom's absence from meals is a benefit. He's taken to wearing this hideous hat, a derby, it's called. It's a blot on my style.

(Jane follows Sally off, up right. Sound: Theme music up and down. Enter Dick down right, with no packages and still wearing the derby.)

DICK

Jane? Not like her to be out just before time to make dinner. Maybe she'll call. What'll I do if the phone rings? It might not be her! I won't answer it. I will, however, have a drink!

(Dick bustles at the table upstage of the couch, produces a glass, sits on the couch. Drinks.)

DICK ()
What a day! May be my last. Or, maybe, I can stretch out life longer. No, this will never work. Well, it might. A little longer. I wonder how!

(Rubs his forehead, snatches off the derby, winces at it. Enter Jane up right.)

JANE
Harry!

(Dick holds the hat over his lap.)

DICK
Jane! How about a drink?

(Jane crosses to center.)

JANE
Since you've started already, why not?

DICK
One stiff drink comin' up!

(Dick scuttles around the end of the couch, ditches hat behind it, bustles with bottle, glasses.)

JANE
You wouldn't believe what I did today.

DICK
Same here! Say, if the phone rings? I'm out.

JANE
I crossed the border!

DICK
Out, gone, away, disappeared.

JANE
I had a look at a house over there.

DICK
Even if your father calls.

JANE
A sort of house and garden show.

DICK
Especially if your father calls.

JANE
Just one house though. This woman I met in that coffee shop in the city-center.

DICK
I had a look at your menu earlier today.

JANE
She has no garden at all.

DICK
So I got some meat out to thaw.

                    JANE
And she seems so cold, so efficient!

                    DICK
Frau Schultz?

                    JANE
No, silly! This woman I met today in the coffee shop. I showed her my garden. And she showed me her house.

                    DICK
Oh, yeah. So, for supper, no need to go pawing around in the freezer in the garage.

                    JANE
Pictures all over in the place.

                    DICK
'Cause dinner is thawing now, in the sink.

                    JANE
Original art, she said. She seems fascinated by style.

                    DICK
Style, hunh?

                    JANE
I know you're hungry. I'll get started cooking as soon as I finish this drink.

                    DICK
And I have to eat and run.

JANE
Harry, you really ought to think about your health!

DICK
I do!

JANE
All this meat!

DICK
Got an important sales meeting tonight.

JANE
You're incorrigible.

DICK
Not quite.

*(Exit both down right.
Sound: Theme music up, down.
Enter Sally down left.)*

SALLY
Tom, in that country, they eat dinner at five in the afternoon! It's hardly even dark out until seven or eight!

(Enter Dick down left.)

SALLY (Cont'd)
So unfashionable! Such a frump!

DICK
Madame Dumont?

SALLY
Have you been listening? I mean this woman I met across the river today. And what quantities they serve! The woman has this huge freezer in her garage!

DICK
Freezer?

SALLY
God know what she keeps in it.

DICK
God knows.

SALLY
She uses all her kitchen scraps to fertilize this interminable garden. She nattered on and on about working the soil and so forth, how the pretty flowers nod knowingly at us.

DICK
Knowingly.

SALLY
A frenzy of anthropomorphizing.

DICK
Say, if the phone rings?

SALLY
I used to day-dream about how cosmopolitan they must be over there!

DICK
If the phone rings? Tell 'em I'm out.

SALLY
What a disappointment when I went! One can just cross over these days, no visa needed at all.

DICK
Gone, away, you haven't seen me. Like it was a mystery?

SALLY
A woman over there. She seemed nice enough. But her style? By the way, I see you've quit wearing that hideous hat!

(Dick slaps his head.)

SALLY (Cont'd)
Good riddance! Glad the woman didn't see it. Though, I must say, she seemed totally insensible to style.

(Enter Jane down right, with empty glass.)

SALLY (Cont'd)
When she was over here, I thought the sight of this place would strike her. I wouldn't have to explain how I have taste and she, poor thing, has none.

(Jane carries her drink around to the back of the couch.)

SALLY (Cont'd)
But she didn't tumble to a thing. Her husband is in electronics sales too. Do you run into a competitor called Harry?

(Jane picks up the hat and stares at it.)

DICK
Coming and going.

(Lights: blackout.)

Act II.

▼

(AT Rise, Lights up. Sound: Theme music up, then segue to café music. Enter Jane up right with a hatbox and a cup and saucer. She sits at right of the table, puts the hatbox on the floor by her chair. She looks off left, and waves.)

JANE
Sally! Sally? I found a free table over here!

(Enter Sally up left with a cup and saucer. On her line she comes to chair left of the table and sits.)

SALLY
Jane, there you are. The phone across the border works like a charm! It's like we were practically next door!

JANE
But we are!

SALLY

All those international tensions made it such a bureaucratic tangle. But today?

JANE

Like the same neighborhood!

SALLY

The same house!

JANE

Uh, that's what I wanted to talk about.

SALLY

I talked to a real estate hustler yesterday! The price he thinks he can get for our house is terrific.

JANE

I have something I want to show you.

SALLY

Have you ever thought about listing yours?

JANE

Sally, have you ever wondered about your husband's hours?

SALLY

I bet you could get a bundle for that place!

JANE
Sally?

SALLY
The market for houses is just booming!

JANE
Haven't you ever been the least bit suspicious?

SALLY
Sure. The day he came back after disappearing for a day on our honeymoon, I hired a detective.

JANE
I hired one the day the honeymoon was over. The detective told me Harry was all work, no play. He made calls on customers, had dinner, went to bed early. Yours?

SALLY
About the same. Totally innocent. Tom did nothing but work.

JANE
The same? Somehow...

SALLY
Somehow the similarity makes me suspicious still.

JANE
Didn't you ever think that maybe he paid off the detective?

SALLY

Sure, but what else was there? Hire a second detective to check up on the first one?

JANE

I asked my Daddy to check up on Harry.

SALLY

I asked my brother. And he seemed to think Tom was okay...

JANE

But still...

SALLY

Still...I'm not sure I can trust my brother. He's in our government.

JANE

My Daddy is in ours. (Pause.) After I met you, and heard about your husband, I was struck by something. You said your husband spends about half the week out on the road. My Harry is gone about three nights a week. Usually Monday, Wednesday, Friday. Sometimes Sunday.

SALLY

Sometimes Sunday. Tom is sometimes gone on Sunday, but not on Monday. Or Wednesday or Friday. He's gone Tuesdays, Thursdays, and Saturdays.

JANE

This antic thought has just dropped into my head. He doesn't chase girls those nights he's out, because...

SALLY
Because he has a steady arrangement?

JANE
You think...?

SALLY
Maybe he's...?

(They make a criss-crossing motion with the index fingers of each hand. They laugh.)

JANE
Oh, no!

SALLY
Surely not.

JANE
Keeping it quiet all these years?

SALLY
Impossible!

JANE
Impossible. Still. I've been wondering about the meaning of this.

(Jane leans over picks up the box to put it on the table.)

SALLY
You brought me a present?

(Jane opens the box, takes out the derby.)

JANE
You may not like it. You complained that your husband assaulted style with a derby. Is he still wearing it?

SALLY
Well, now that you mention it...

JANE
Did he have it yesterday?

SALLY
I think he left the house with it.

JANE
And when he came back? Of course, there are lots of hats like this in the world. But this was Harry's...

(Jane sniffs the hat. Sally takes the hat, sniffs it.)

SALLY
It's his. It's Tom's. Where did you find it?

JANE
My place. By the phone. Just after Harry scooted out of there. Or Tom.

(Enter Dick up left or right. He wears a dark rain coat, a bandanna over his brows, dark glasses.)

                    SALLY
I keep waiting for the earth to open and swallow me.

                    JANE
I keep waiting for the alarm to go off and wake me up from this.

(Dick eases into up center seat. From here on the director must devise movements—anywhere across the stage—to eliminate a static picture.)

                    DICK
Ladies.

                    SALLY
You're not invited!

                    JANE
How rude!

(Dick lifts his sunglasses.)

                    DICK
Hey, it's me.

                    JANE
Harry!

                    SALLY
Tom!

                    DICK
Shh!

                    JANE
But you—

                    SALLY
Are you?

                    DICK
I'm me!

                    JANE
But which?

                    SALLY
Tom?

                    JANE
Harry?

                    SALLY
Or both?
            (Dick dons the hat.)

                    DICK
The very same!

                    JANE
You bastard!

                    DICK

Shush!

                    JANE

Why shush now?

        (Dick thrusts the hat into the box.)

                    DICK

I'm sub-rosa!

                    SALLY

Now who?

                    DICK

Persona non grata!

                    JANE

What do you mean?

                    DICK

Non compos mentis, too!

                    SALLY

What's going on?

                    DICK

Quiet! No one knows I'm here!

        (They all look around.)

                    JANE

They're ignoring us.

DICK
I hope so. Listen! I'm dead.

SALLY
You don't look it.

DICK
Jane, if I'm not dead, I'll be executed as a spy. I was hired by her brother to be one. He got me visas to cross the border. Selling electronic parts on this side of the border was my cover!

SALLY
This better be good!

DICK
Sally, I was hired by her father, too, to be a spy, too. He got me visas to cross over. Buying cheap electronic parts on that side of the border was my cover.

JANE
You had visas from both governments?

DICK
Visas, visas, I coulda sold 'em like raffle tickets!

SALLY
But who are you?

DICK
They're listening over there?

(Sally rises, exits up left.)

JANE
Are you my Harry? Or her Tom?

DICK
Sure!

JANE
Sure of what?

DICK
Be calm!

(Sally re-enters, sits.)

SALLY
They are listening, but not us.

JANE
To what?

SALLY
Something intellectual, neo-post structuralist digestion. Has that any meaning?

DICK
We have to be careful.

SALLY
You have to be careful!

DICK
We all do! Listen, it's complicated.

JANE
Are you married to me? Or to her?

SALLY
If you're not Tom, who are you?

DICK
Sure thing, don't worry about it.

JANE
Worry? I want to know if I have a husband.

SALLY
If I can hope for a pension!

(Dick gestures.)

DICK
That's it!

JANE
What's it!

SALLY
Where?

(Both women look around.)

DICK
Here! Your pensions! Remember Frau Schultz! Madame Dumont!

JANE
Why?

SALLY
What for?

DICK
They lost their pensions!

SALLY
Mister Schultz was a spy!

JANE
Mister Dumont was a traitor!

DICK
They were each of them the gonzo, the fall guy, the sap left holding the bag at the end of the snipe hunt!

SALLY
Clearly they were fools.

DICK
One for trusting your brother and the other for trusting your father!

JANE

What did Daddy ever do?

SALLY

Or my brother George!

DICK

Nothing. They hired a goon to do it for them. Felton. Ever hear of him?

JANE

No.

SALLY

He plays center half for Manchester United?

DICK

He's a professional assassin!

JANE

Have you been going to movies?

SALLY

Where do you hear such stuff?

DICK

I was in the same meeting as George when it was decided to have Felton terminate Dumont. Your Daddy would have had to approve it for Felton to terminate Schultz.

JANE

How much television have you been watching?

DICK
I spotted Felton a day ago, twice. He was tracking me. I called George about it. Now that peace has broken out, I know too much. George assured me that he and the whole government had only the best intentions toward me.

SALLY
That snake! That scum-bag! My brother can't be trusted.

DICK
Jane, Walter said the very same words to me.

JANE
But how can you be sure this Felton is stalking you?

DICK
Two points! Number one is the bodies. Schultz and Dumont both were killed by Felton. Felton always leaves the clothes on the bodies, and the papers, but cuts off the head and the hands, sends them to his client, to prove he got the right person.

JANE
But just because—

DICK
Number two! I caught him in our garage, with a silenced pistol, waiting for me behind our garbage cans.

JANE
What did he say?

DICK

Not much. We grunted at each other as we struggled. I have his body now in our freezer. In my clothes. I had to move some packages of meat, and ice cream, into the kitchen fridge. You wouldn't believe how hard it is to put fresh underpants on a dead man.

JANE

Fresh underpants? Why?

DICK

My underpants. My clothing. My papers.

(Dick opens his raincoat to show his suit.)

SALLY

How awful! That suit doesn't fit at all!

DICK

It's Felton's! Once the body was stiff enough, I cut off the head, and the hands, so the body will look like his own m.o.

SALLY

I think I get it. In your clothing?

DICK

And with my papers in the pockets. I'm carrying Felton's now.

JANE
But who are you? What's your name?

(Dick produces a breast-pocket wallet.)

DICK
Allow me to introduce myself. Felton's the name. Bruce Felton.

SALLY
Bruce!

DICK
Yes?

SALLY
Loathsome name. I hate it.

DICK
It'll take some getting used to.

JANE
It'll never work!

DICK
Sure, it'll work.

SALLY
Right! Long enough to get a plane ticket is all you need.

JANE
When he's gone there's no way they can say he's here!

SALLY

And when the bureaucrats deny our pensions? What then?

JANE

They wouldn't dare!

SALLY

They stiffed Madame Dumont.

DICK

And Frau Schultz.

JANE

That's right!
DICK
Because the bureaucrats had a positive i.d. of each body. But if my stunt works, they'll wait forever for an i.d.

SALLY

Why?

DICK

Jane's kitchen doesn't have a disposall.

JANE

I compost.

DICK

So I took the head and hands across the border. Piece of cake. Don't even need a visa these days. Ground them up in your kitchen.

                    SALLY
Grotesque!

                    DICK
It was. Took forever. The hands went okay, but a whole skull? And the teeth didn't grind at all. I still have 'em on me. Like a pocketful of chicklets.

                    JANE
When you proposed, you said you loved me!

                    DICK
What?

                    SALLY
Told me that too.

                    DICK
Let's not get side-tracked!

                    JANE
If you loved me, why did you marry her?

                    DICK
This will never work. I married her because Walter said I had to.

                    JANE
Daddy did? Why?

DICK
Because her brother's in the government over there.

SALLY
You never loved me?

DICK
Don't say never! By the time the kids got used to me, I did!

SALLY
But you married her first?

DICK
Not quite. I married her that same afternoon!

SALLY
Why?

DICK
Because your brother said I had to.

JANE
What?

SALLY
Why?

DICK
Figure it out. Her father was in the Interior Ministry in those days. Still is. He's the minister!

JANE

Didn't you ever love me?

DICK

Of course I did. Still do! Cute girl like you? And a great cook!

SALLY

You can't love us both!

DICK

Why not? I'm a guy. Guys are different from girls.

SALLY

You loved her more!

DICK

I knew this wouldn't work. Listen, finance, not romance is the issue for you now. We need two widows at two funerals.

SALLY

For whom?

DICK

For your husband! The cops find a body by the river, the head and the hands missing, and the cops know right away it means that's Felton's calling card. So George doesn't worry, Walter doesn't worry for a few days, neither worries right away that he doesn't get a styrofoam mail parcel packed in dry ice, yet. Both of 'em figure, because it's Felton's m.o., a body in my clothes, my papers, that I'm the body, and that Felton is lying low a while.

SALLY
But when they check the DNA?

DICK
The DNA! Our state pathologist couldn't run a Wassermann test with enough accuracy to keep Our Glorious Leader from dying a miserable and well-deserved death from venereal disease! DNA! That lab cannot count high enough to fill a prescription! That's why this damned peace has broken out, thanks to the old goat's death!

SALLY
But don't both George and her Daddy know?

JANE
That they married us both to you?

DICK
All those guys have ever known is stuff I've been telling them.

SALLY
But they're bound to find out—

DICK
They're not bound to find out anything.

JANE
How stupid are they?

DICK
Not stupid, just slow. Sitting in a committee meeting, they can argue a point, but thinking on their feet?

SALLY
Like you do.

DICK
Like I'm trying to do now!

JANE
But how can we have a funeral?

SALLY
A body in the casket with no head on it?

DICK
And what did Frau Schultz do? Madame Dumont?

JANE
Cremation?

SALLY
It's so tasteless.

DICK
Tasteful, Full! Change your standards, Sally! Your pension depends on it.

JANE
So I have the body cremated over here?

SALLY
How can I have it cremated over there?

DICK
I'll cut you off a chunk.

JANE
But you have to have the body left by the river.

DICK
So Sally can cremate something else, a dog, a goat! Jane, you have a freezer full of meat in the garage! Be creative! Do I have to think of everything? (Pause) But you're both right.

JANE
About what?

DICK
I can hear you thinking. The gears grinding. You're right. It's never gonna work. I have to die sooner or later in any case. What the hell. It certainly would be more relaxing to be dead.

SALLY
What'll I tell the boys?

JANE
The girls?

DICK
You'll think of something. What are you going to say to your brother? To your father?

SALLY
Surely we can work something that will fool the bureaucrats.

JANE
What's-his-name here fooled us for years.

SALLY
We can work a scam as well as he can!

JANE
It'd be a shame to lose the pension. I'd love to finish the house.

SALLY
I could travel.

JANE
Finish the garden.

SALLY
See Europe. America.

JANE
Maybe we can work something out.

SALLY
It's awful. But we have to work on something.

                    DICK
It'll never work.

           (Blackout. Exit all.
  Lights: up half, vertical, institutional.
  Enter up right, George, Walter, Jane, Sally.)

                    SALLY
We think you two ought to meet each other.

                    JANE
In the same fix, more or less.

                    SALLY
You know of each other, of course. My brother George here is, or used to be, our Foreign Affairs Minster.

                    JANE
And Daddy here used to be our Minister of the Interior.

                    GEORGE
Walter.

                    WALTER
George. Awkward to meet under such circumstances.

                    GEORGE
Unfortunate.

                    WALTER
They have me on the stand every afternoon.

GEORGE
Me too, on our side of the river.

WALTER
Damned scandal.

GEORGE
These law-suits are ridiculous.

WALTER
A perversion of justice. And just for a pension!

GEORGE
If the idiots on your side of the river hadn't denied a pension to Schultz's widow, there wouldn't have been any lawsuit.

WALTER
And Madame Dupont's pension? What folly suggested that you deny hers?

GEORGE
Yours! That's where we got the idea.

WALTER
A saving of budgetary excess, I suppose?

GEORGE
That was the excuse. In fact, the budget is in tatters. Expenses are way over income.

WALTER
The budget, of course, is always the real reason for such nonsense.

GEORGE
We'll just have to grin and bear it until it all blows over.

WALTER
Tie everything down until the seas grow calm.

JANE
The storm may be a little too fierce, Daddy, just to let it work itself out.

GEORGE
It's not just the nonsense in the courts, but the hysteria in the newspapers!

SALLY
Ad-volume is way up. It's a commercial wind-fall.

WALTER
I told our police chief to close those papers down. And he said he couldn't do it. Against the law, he said!

JANE
They only printed the truth.

WALTER
Against the law! Mark that! From a policeman, the chief! Against the law!

SALLY
Mark that.

WALTER
He never paid the law the least attention before! Now, suddenly—

GEORGE
It's the death of your Glorious Leader that is at the root of all these problems.

WALTER
Well, as for him, good riddance.

GEORGE
But he kept things solid. Permanent.

WALTER
Whole damned society is in flux.

SALLY
All my sons have left the country, taken new jobs. Your stupidity makes it hard for them to get any work here.

GEORGE
My stupidity?

SALLY
Everyone is blaming you.

GEORGE
You too, I suppose!

JANE
Daddy! Your granddaughters feel glad that their names got changed when they married.

SALLY
George, if you had to leave the country, where would we go?

GEORGE
Leave? I'm not going to leave!

WALTER
Why would we leave?

GEORGE
Those two lawyers are suing the two governments, not us.

JANE
You are each a star witness.

SALLY
And the chief scapegoats.

GEORGE
How do you make that out?

SALLY
The publicity.

JANE
The newspapers.

WALTER

Oh, pooh! This time next week they will have some other scandal to feast on.

(Exit Walter up right.)

GEORGE

He's right, Sally. No one is going to pay attention to this nonsense for long.

(Exit George up right.)

SALLY

They're in denial.

JANE

You've been traveling. You pick out a place.

SALLY

Come, help me choose. Some place warm, would be best.

(Exit up right, Sally and Jane.
Lights: bright sunny lighting for a scene in Latin America. The table has a bright cloth, a bowl of red punch, with a dipper and pitcher; both the couches have bright throws.
Everyone wears sandals or spadrilles, sunglasses.
The waiter, Camarero, wears black pants, a light shirt with huge ruffled sleeves, like a member of a mariachi band, and bright bandanna covering his head. Any beard, mustache, eyebrows are black.
The other two men wear shorts and very loud shirts.

*The two ladies wear huge multicolored mumus.
Sound: A constant background of latin music.
Enter Camarero with a tray, putting glasses on the table.
He gestures toward off left.
Enter George and Walter.)*

CAMARERO
As Camarero promised, with a view! Will this do, señores?

WALTER
Just fine, Camarero.

CAMARERO
When Camarero promises, Camarero delivers!

GEORGE
This is great. Nice view.

CAMARERO
Camarero promised the hors d'oeuvres. Next to be delivered!

*(Exit Camarero up right.
Walter gestures toward up left.)*

WALTER
Jane, Sally? Over here.

(Enter Jane, Sally up left.)

GEORGE
Hey, Sally, get a load of this view!

(George gestures at audience.)

SALLY
No need to sell it, George. You don't own it.

JANE
It's very nice, George.

WALTER
I confess it does not take my mind off what might be happening back home.

JANE
It's no concern of yours any longer, Daddy.

WALTER
The present minister is too young for the job.

GEORGE
Walter, some young buck would have taken over as your Interior minister sooner or later.

(Re-enter Camarero up left with a tray of hors d'oeuvres.)

WALTER
All those years in the ministry, and now...

GEORGE
I know, I feel the same way.

CAMARERO
A snack, señores?

JANE
Oh, goody!

(They each take a piece.)

SALLY
Little pieces of bread. With mysterious gobs.

WALTER
Still, they don't taste bad.

GEORGE
When this trip is over, I might go back.

SALLY
What for?

GEORGE
Get into politics again.

SALLY
Politics! You should be cured of that by now.

(Camarero returns the tray to the table, pours punch into glasses, serves the glasses around, ladies first.)

GEORGE
Go back have a look around. After this vacation.

SALLY
Vacation!

CAMARERO
A glass of sangria, señora? Good for the blood!

GEORGE
An elective office, perhaps.

SALLY
You're delusional!

GEORGE
Why?

JANE
The newspapers in your country, George.

CAMARERO
A glass of sangria, señores?

JANE
And your opponents for election. They all would have lots to say, to print.

SALLY
Your history in the Foreign office would offer juicy material.

GEORGE
Just on account of that one widow?

SALLY
You're not on vacation, George! You're in exile.

GEORGE
That woman and her damned law-suit.

SALLY
She had to get her pension back. What did she have to lose?

JANE
Camarero? What is this?

CAMARERO
A bit of fruit juice, señora. And some spirits.

SALLY
What's it called?

CAMARERO
Sangria. As if it were blood. It is but a mild tonic.

JANE
It's refreshing.

CAMARERO
Taken in moderation, señora. A refill? Of course! A little moderation, señora, is too much of a good thing!

SALLY
Are you a poet?

CAMARERO
A poet? Never! I utterly deny it.

JANE

A philosopher then?

CAMARERO

Guilty, señora, to my shame if I had any.

WALTER

The ladies have a point, my boy, about going back.

GEORGE

You're in same boat as me, Walter!

WALTER

Alas, yes. Frau Schultz's lawsuit—

GEORGE

She tied a can to your tail!

WALTER

Madame Dumont tied one to yours, George.

SALLY

He deserved it.

WALTER

Does anyone deserve the malicious humiliation of that trial?

JANE

Those trials.

GEORGE
That media circus pushed aside matters of state!

WALTER
We might have been on the verge of war!

SALLY
War! Meaningless postures!

WALTER
The honor of a nation at stake! That's not meaningless!

SALLY
An excuse to send young men to kill each other so everyone at headquarters can get his name in the papers!

GEORGE
Any person in authority is forced to make hard decisions!

JANE
The usual meaningless excuse.

GEORGE
I was concerned about national security!

SALLY
Nonsense, you sought to save, not the nation, but your next promotion.

JANE
And that inane defense that you cooked up for your trial! Just because Tom and Harry both were salesman, you both tried to claim they were one man.

WALTER
Dammit, they were!

JANE
When those lawyers asked you to explain how we had two funerals, you sat there with your faces hanging out.

SALLY
The mere idea that they were one man, hired by each of you to spy on the other, made you look like a pair of boobies.

JANE
What a preposterous story!

SALLY
No one believed it! (Aside to Jane.) Thank god!

WALTER
That damned trial!

JANE
A nonsensical piece of work! (Aside to Sally.) Or we might have had to sue for our pensions!

WALTER
I never got to show how things looked to before the Leader died, not after!

GEORGE
His death was such a relief.

SALLY
And Tom's? That was a relief too, right?

GEORGE
Don't take it wrong!

SALLY
Tom was a wonderful man! My boys loved him!

JANE
My girls loved Harry!

SALLY
They were both wonderful men!

(About here the women reach their climax of tearful rage.)

JANE
Did you really have to have them killed?

SALLY
By that Fulton, Farfel, something like that.

WALTER
Felton.

GEORGE
Bruce Felton.

SALLY
And where is he? You never bothered to produce him at your trials.

GEORGE

We tried!

SALLY

Frau Schultz's lawyers made mincemeat of your fantasies.

JANE

Madame Dupont's lawyer made you both into national laughing stocks!

SALLY

But getting Tom killed is a crime for which you'll never be punished!

JANE

Getting Harry killed—my girls would never forgive grandpa if they knew!

SALLY

I could so easily hate you! Even if you are my own brother!

JANE

I try to make allowances, Daddy. What did the judge call you at the trial, an old fool? A phony pretentious, windbag?

WALTER

I couldn't help it!

SALLY

Always a convenient excuse.

JANE
I try to forget your excuses Daddy. Instead I just keep your defects in mind.

GEORGE
Why did you come on this vacation then?

SALLY
I like to remind you of your sins.

GEORGE
Can't we give it a rest?

(The women move near one couch.)

JANE
You still think about him?

(The men move near the other couch.)

WALTER
Damned case doesn't bear thinking about, boy.

SALLY
My Tom?

GEORGE
Mine or yours?

JANE
Or my Harry?

WALTER
Either one, really.

(Camarero hovers with the pitcher; he has been refilling glasses left and right. Gradually the women, the men sit on their respective couches.)

SALLY
Well, which was which?

JANE
He felt so real!

GEORGE
If only we could have brought Felton to the surface, to testify.

SALLY
He was real enough. But which one was he?

WALTER
Felton will never reappear. He went to deep cover. Never sent us any evidence for his last job, you know.

JANE
Maybe he was the third one all along.

GEORGE
Not to us either. Never sent us his bill.

SALLY
Maybe he didn't just adopt that Felton identity.

JANE
He was Felton all along?

WALTER
Felton. Hardly likely to testify willingly. But what a man!

SALLY
But Tom was capable of that! On the spur of the moment!

GEORGE
He was a piece of work! No chance to get him to talk. The new rules mean that a judge cannot admit forced testimony.

JANE
I'd like to talk to him. Just once.

WALTER
Not like the old days.

SALLY
Not a chance, Jane.

GEORGE
Damned inconvenient.

JANE
Gone. Like my first husband.

WALTER
That county is a mess these days. I wouldn't like it. Wouldn't go back if I could.

SALLY
Mine too.

GEORGE
Things have changed.

JANE
I wouldn't take back my first husband back, though.

WALTER
They will soon have as much trouble as the Americans do.

JANE
Not after Harry.

GEORGE
You think it will be that bad?

SALLY
No regrets?

WALTER
When the police have to obey the law?

JANE
Only that he's gone.

GEORGE
That is a shocking change.

SALLY
Whoever he was, Tom was a piece of work. Great while he lasted.

WALTER
Police hog-tied by the law! Hard to get anything done that way.

JANE
We're facing our twilight years, I'm afraid.

GEORGE
Still, they seem to work things out.

SALLY
Sounds depressing.

WALTER
Not for long! Mark my words. We're well out of it, George.

GEORGE
Maybe. But I'd go back if I could.

JANE
Nice to have Harry as long as I did.

WALTER
But you can't.

GEORGE
Well, not yet.

SALLY
Yeah, Tom, too. But now that's over, what's the point?

CAMARERO
It's like meaning. Whatever I intend when I say something, my intention never matches whatever you interpret from what I said.

JANE
Whaaaaat?

SALLY
What do you mean?

CAMARERO
That's what I mean! My life cannot make a point, unless some others see a point to it. It's like personality, too.

GEORGE
Now it's personality?

CAMARERO
Your personality is not the real you, inside you!

WALTER
It certainly is!

CAMARERO
No one can know the inner you. The real you inside there is like certain gods. No name!

SALLY

What's your point?

CAMARERO

Patience, my dears. Trust me. The word, "personality" is only a word. It does not mean you, but it means all the ways everyone treats you. Their opinion of you is your personality. You cannot command it. Only the others can. You can change it, you can decide to affect others differently, and it takes time, but you can do it.

WALTER

Impertinent and irrelevant!

GEORGE

No, no. Maybe he's got—gimme an example!

CAMARERO

Take me, for example. For many years I was scoundrel, well, perhaps, only a rascal.

JANE

I believe it.

CAMARERO

One not taken by others as a man who contributes to the good of society. Now, however, I am a waiter. No longer am I am a rascal, but of use!

SALLY

Everyone loves you.

CAMARERO

This is true. Now, when I die, they can say of my life, that it had a point. Camarero brought drinks, brought little pieces of bread mounted with mysterious gobs. Something at least to write on the head stone. What are they going to write on yours?

WALTER

By then I will not care.

CAMARERO

But that is also true for Alexander the Great! For Julius Caesar!

GEORGE

For Dumont!

WALTER

For Schultz!

JANE

Harry!

SALLY

Tom!

JANE

Disappeared!

SALLY

Swallowed up!

CAMARERO
We eat such wonderful meals, to give a meaning to the lives of otherwise anonymous cows, lambs, fish, chickens! Sweet cakes, too! An aesthetic experience. Then we, in turn, conquer the world to make a nice breakfast for anonymous worms.

SALLY
That's a cheery thought!

CAMARERO
Don't be depressed, my dears! Look at the nice view.

(Camarero retreats to the table, reloads his pitcher.)

GEORGE
This guy is a piece of work!

JANE
Camarero reminds me...

SALLY
Me too!

GEORGE
Makes me think of someone.

WALTER
Yes, yes, who was it?

JANE
Of?

SALLY

Of him!

WALTER

Of Felton?

JANE

You think it's him, in disguise?

GEORGE

No, of the other guy. The salesman!

SALLY

No, couldn't be.

WALTER

Yes, you're right!

JANE

We're delusional.

WALTER

If only we could have brought him to the surface.

SALLY

Ever time I see an interesting guy—

GEORGE

We might have managed in that trial—

JANE

You think maybe it's him.

WALTER
It's too late to think about what might have been.

SALLY
You too!

GEORGE
Exile's bad.

JANE
Me too. We're condemned to do that for the rest of our lives.

WALTER
But it's better than jail for life.

(Camarero returns to refill glasses.)

CAMARERO
What is the meaning of this view? It wasn't put there merely to give us pleasure. It was not put there at all. It is a chance concurrence of landscape, sea-scape, sky, light. But it does give us pleasure. Why, my dears, must it need a meaning? Why, then, do we?

(Lights: dimming to red.)

JANE
It can't be him.

CAMARERO

We can never return to our past. We race with as much speed as one could hope to an eventual death. The present, however, might entertain us. About now the dinner waiters arrive.

(The four on the couches grunt, struggling without success to rise.)

SALLY

It might be him!

CAMARERO

But you, I suspect, are unable to move yourselves to the dining room. Paralyzed by sangria! I count a stiffening number of re-fills!

(Lights: Shift to purple.)

JANE

I have to know!

CAMARERO

Soon I will bring the tray, more little pieces of bread with the mysterious gobs. You will not starve. You will survive the night. You will awake here at three, or four, in the morning, stiff, conscious of your age. It's only one life and one death! One to a customer! So, don't take it so seriously!

(Lights: Shift to blue.)

SALLY

How can we know?

CAMARERO

And now the last glows of twilight. Hasn't this been fun?

(Lights: suddenly up full.)

JANE

Get his pants off!

CAMARERO

So aesthetic! Such style!

(Sound: latin theme to rapid beat. Jane and Sally with feline grace rise, approach Camarero.)

SALLY

Philosophic bullshit!

(Sally and Jane try to grab. Camarero. He avoids them. A general scrum follows.)

CAMARERO

Ladies, please!

JANE

Grab him!

SALLY

Hold him down!

GEORGE

Sally!

WALTER

Jane, what are you doing!

SALLY

It's him!

JANE

I know it's him!

(Camarero escapes them.)

CAMARERO

I insist, I'm me!

WALTER

This shocking behavior, sir!

CAMARERO

I quite agree, señor! Do the ladies want to see me au nature?

SALLY

Birth mark!

(Jane and Sally tackle Camarero again.)

JANE

Down here!

SALLY
Shaped like the map of Poland!

(Camarero escapes again.)

CAMARERO
A slavic application. How vulgar!

JANE
I thought it looked more like the map of Bulgaria!

CAMARERO
Balkan? Never! I am disgraced by the association.

(Camarero exits on the run, up right.)

SALLY
He's gone!

JANE
Damn, this will never work!

SALLY
Have to catch him!

(Sally and Jane prowl toward up right.)

JANE
Wait!

SALLY
For what?

JANE

If it is him, will we lose our pensions?

SALLY

Ouch! That's a thought!

JANE

Don't be in too much of a hurry! As for me, I'll take my chances!

(Jane exits up right.)

SALLY

Not alone, you won't!

(Sally exits up right.)

GEORGE

What the hell?

WALTER

George! Help me up! Did I miss something?

GEORGE

They went that way.

(Exit George and Walter up right. Lights: blackout.)